MW00479328

GOOD DECISIONS EQUAL SUCCESS

STOP DECISION ANXIETY
AND START TAKING ACTION

GOOD
DECISIONS

SUCCESS

KANDIS PORTER and **DAMON LEMBI**

LIONCREST
PUBLISHING

GOOD DECISIONS EQUAL SUCCESS
Stop Decision Anxiety and Start Taking Action

FIRST EDITION

ISBN   978-1-5445-3994-2   *Hardcover*
       978-1-5445-3993-5   *Paperback*
       978-1-5445-3992-8   *Ebook*

*To Cara, my constant support and partner in all of life's
adventures. Marrying you was the best decision I ever
made. Thank you for being the love of my life.*

—DAMON

To My Dearest Husband, My Dad, and My Grandpa Chuck:

*Thank you for always being there for me and guiding me toward
rational decision-making. This book is dedicated to you, for
always being my steady in a constantly changing world.*

—KANDIS

CONTENTS

INTRODUCTION

WHEN THE WEATHER IS BAD, AN AIR FORCE WEATHER
forecaster feels it. And hears it. The phone in the Operational
Weather Squadron (OWS) never stops ringing. They answer
stressful calls while keeping their eyes on the Aviation Routine
Weather Reports (METARs). With storms on the horizon, they
work impossibly tight timelines to update forecasts.

Get it wrong, and the ripple effect from a bad decision will
impact thousands.

Weather forecasters for the Air Force have to thoroughly
analyze data and predict the near-term future quickly, under
pressure, with millions of dollars of equipment and human
lives on the line. They have to make objective, data-based
decisions, based on the information they have—no matter how
lacking that information may be. They are also responsible
for the DD Form 175-1, the Flight Weather Briefing. In it, they
document winds, cloud coverage and levels, thunderstorms,
turbulence, icing, temperatures, altitude, freezing levels—any
weather event of note. Pilots make life-and-death decisions
based on the information provided in that form. When people

are jumping out of planes and you are trying to complete a mission, this information is critical.

It's a high-pressure gig.

By the time Kandis, one of the authors of this book, left Scott Air Force Base after her tour of duty as a weather forecaster, she had issued 724 weather warnings with 96 percent accuracy, providing resource protection for $10 billion in government assets over a twenty-two state region. Without her due diligence, the weather had the potential to destroy not only billions of dollars of assets but could also lead to loss of life.

Kandis had to critically think under pressure. Her job taught her to go "all in" when making decisions and gave her the confidence to know when she was making the right call. Did she get it right 100 percent of the time? Absolutely not. Although she always used data when justifying her reasoning and was open to changing course, when needed.

The Air Force is highly strategic and targeted in how it trains its forecasters to make decisions. After all, their decisions provide the foundation for much of the Air Force's decision-making and operations. Key to the Air Force's approach is making decisions from *objective criteria* rather than emotions, regardless of the time pressure or stakes involved. No matter how much a pilot in North Dakota wants to take off with a clean weather briefing, the weather forecaster in Illinois must remain focused on the facts. On the leisurely side, it is no fun being the weather forecaster issuing a warning when lightning occurs within a five-nautical mile radius of an Air Force championship softball game, causing it to be postponed or canceled. But it is important.

Objective criteria and a decision-making *process* lead to better outcomes. Decisions based on "gut feelings" crash and burn. In the Air Force, with lives on the line, that's not a risk anyone is willing to take.

A LEARNED BEHAVIOR

Decision-making is a critical skill, especially for leaders.[1] The quality of the decisions you make will determine the quality of your work and personal life. Good decisions will get you more of what you want: happiness, money, promotions, peace of mind, good relationships, and wise investments. A string of bad decisions will do the opposite. Choosing the right marketing director, or life partner, will have an immensely positive impact on your life. Choosing the wrong one...well, we all know how that story ends. Good decisions really do equal success.

Though in every decision, no matter how good, there's an element of luck. Sometimes, no matter how much you prepare, good decisions lead to bad consequences. Or vice versa. Say you're running late. You think you can squeak past that yellow light in time, but it turns red before you get there. Instantly there's a decision in front of you: if all goes well you'll make it to your destination on time, no harm no foul. But if luck turns the other direction? You'll regret that decision for years to come, whether it be a ticket for running a red light or worse, with consequences of injury or even loss of life. Not every good decision will turn out perfectly, but sooner or later the bad ones *will* catch up with you.

The good and the bad news is that decision-making is a learned behavior. No one is born knowing how to do it. You might have heard the saying, "Practice makes progress." If you practice and learn, you will get better at decision-making over time, and make better decisions. By being intentional, and applying a sound process, you'll reach successful outcomes far more often.

---

1   *In this book, we are speaking to leaders, people who have responsibility for or influence over other people. In many cases, leaders are executives and managers. In other cases, they are team leads, or individual contributors whose voices have weight. Leaders think innovatively. If you are reading this book, you are likely a leader in some significant way, and so we are speaking to you.*

Kandis credits the Air Force's extensive training for changing the way she thinks about high-impact decision-making. Damon, the other author of this book, credits his experience growing his company, Learnit, to a multi-million dollar thriving business, and being forced to make constant high-impact decisions with his and others' livelihoods. We've had to learn and grow, just like we hope you'll learn and grow. We continue to work at decision-making to this day. It's not a perfect science, but once you've gotten comfortable with the process, you'll never have to "fly blind" again.

MAKING DECISIONS IN ORGANIZATIONS

High-impact decisions are tricky in all parts of life, and the process we outline will be useful in a variety of situations, personal and professional. However, this book is primarily concerned with leaders making decisions at work, and we chose our examples and our topics of discussion accordingly.

Organizational decision-making is particularly challenging and can get messy. There are conflicts of interest and competing priorities that will eat you alive if you're not prepared. Mid-level managers in particular can get caught between stakeholders, as they try to thread the needle between many competing needs. A strong structure for decision-making is critical under these circumstances. It provides confidence. It helps you cut through the noise to focus on what's truly important.

A 2020 episode of the *McKinsey Podcast* reports that 40 percent of an executive's time is spent making decisions.[2] The

---

2   Aaron De Smet, Leigh Weiss, and Simon London, "To Unlock Better Decision Making, Plan Better Meetings," November 9, 2020, in *The McKinsey Podcast*, podcast, 40:54, https://www.mckinsey.com/capabilities/people-and-organizational-performance/our-insights/to-unlock-better-decision-making-plan-better-meetings.

time you invest in making better decisions will pay off tremendously, day by day, in the quality of the results you're able to achieve. The more senior you get in your career, the more important decisions become.

A STEP-BY-STEP PROCESS

High-impact decisions should never be made from emotion, assumptions (that aren't stress tested), or your gut.

That's worth saying one more time: high-impact decisions should *never* be made from **emotion**, **assumptions**, or your **gut**.

We call that, "rolling the dice," and it leads to poor decisions more often than it doesn't. Instead, decisions should be made with an intentional process, based on in-depth thinking and detailed information.

To quote Thomas Jefferson, "I'm a great believer in luck. And I find the harder I work, the more I have of it." A good decision-making process will bring you more luck and more success. A good process gives you the confidence and structure you need to make better high-impact decisions. We'll teach you our process, step by step, in this book.

First, let's define what we mean by a "high-impact decision." A high-impact decision is an important decision that's difficult to reverse. For example, if a company decides to expand its retail footprint in many new locations, it will most likely sign contracts for the retail spaces that are difficult to get out of. The money will be committed. That's an important decision and difficult to reverse. Similarly, if you're hiring and passing on a potential candidate for a senior role, they will likely accept another job before you can return to offer the job again. They will be gone. That's also an important decision and difficult to reverse.

Not every decision you make is high impact. If you order an item on the menu at a restaurant and it's no good, that's unfortunate, but it's not going to impact the rest of your week. If you have coffee with someone on a dating app and it goes badly, you've lost an hour and had a cup of coffee. Hiring the wrong marketing assistant will not alter your business in the same way that hiring the wrong Chief Marketing Officer would.

WHO WE ARE

As you now know, Kandis spent years as a weather forecaster in the Air Force and eventually became a Captain and worked at the Pentagon. Both of these positions required making high-impact, rapid-fire decisions on the clock. In 2010, she moved to a well-known consulting company, working for large federal agencies, and eventually in 2016 opened her own boutique management consulting company. She now teaches decision-making at an Advanced Leadership Academy at a university.

Kandis has lived and breathed decision-making for decades, not only on the job for the Air Force but also in running her own business. Consultants see every possible permutation of organizational decision-making: the good, the bad, and the ugly—and Kandis is no exception. She's worked with clients to turn bad situations into good ones, over and over, and has developed specific and structured tools to help.

Damon has been the Chief Executive Officer (CEO) of Learnit for twenty-eight years. Learnit is a learning and development organization that has positively impacted millions of leaders. The pace of change in the learning industry since the 1990s has been intense. Damon has made a number of excellent decisions to adapt and evolve the company to keep up with the changing technology and environment and has outlasted multiple competitors.

As a leader, Damon has made thousands and thousands of decisions for the business. He will also be the first to tell you that earlier in his career, he made business decisions without thinking them through, and took many unnecessary gambles. Since Learnit's motto is to be a "learn-it-all rather than a know-it-all," Damon has learned from every bad decision and is happy to share the hard-won lessons in these pages, so that you can learn from his mistakes and successes. (To learn even more about Damon's journey, check out his book, *The Learn-It-All Leader*.)

Damon and Kandis see eye-to-eye as business owners in so many different ways. They are both logical and driven to solve problems by creating processes. They emphasize learning and drive, and they respect each other's input and strengths. Damon has amazing, creative, ideas, and Kandis is profoundly practical and detail-oriented. They are force multipliers for each other. They provide mutual mentorship, and they make better decisions together than they ever could apart.

WHAT TO EXPECT

This book will teach you how to think smarter. It will teach you to make better decisions, both personally and professionally, through a practical process and specific, actionable tools.

Part One of this book will provide general principles to help improve your decision-making across the board. You'll learn common mistakes of decision-making, the mindset shift that will lead to better decisions and the biggest reason why decision-making in organizations gets messy. (Spoiler alert: it's all about a misunderstanding of decision roles.) Part One will be helpful whether the decision you face is high or low impact. For truly high-impact decisions, on the other hand, you'll want to use the rigorous and in-depth process of decision-making in Part Two. The process will take too much time to invest in every decision, but for critical ones that are hard to reverse, it's well worth the extra effort.

Part Two contains tools and a step-by-step process for better high-impact decisions, and will make up the majority of the book.

This book is not a quick fix to a bad situation. It is a tactical book on the specifics of how to make decisions. There are stories and examples to help bring the points home (many of these are from Damon; he's the storyteller of the duo).

This book is not about mathematical techniques used to estimate the possible outcomes of an uncertain event such as Monte Carlo simulations, and it's not about theory, as there are many other fine theoretical resources out there. Instead, this is a practical book for everyday leaders, to help them make the right decisions under pressure in high-impact situations.

This book is primarily intended for leaders who are making strategic, budgetary, and structural decisions or are involved in making calls regarding systems and processes. It's also for anyone who wants to be more thoughtful about the decisions they make to achieve better outcomes.

Good decisions really do equal success.

START TAKING ACTION

Have you ever had this experience...?

Your mind is racing. Your stomach hurts, and you feel anxious. You can feel the flop-sweat coming on. You know you need to make a major decision, and you're up at three in the morning worried about it. You *can* stop the stressful churning, make a decision, and take action you feel good about.

Before we share our process for *how* to stop the churning and decide, we want to back up and alert you to the most common potholes in decision-making. These aren't little bumps in the road. If you hit one of those potholes, your car is going to be torn up. If, on the other hand, you avoid these mistakes, you could take *literally* none of the other advice in this book and still be ahead of the game. Read on to find out how.

PART ONE

HUMAN FACTORS IN DECISION-MAKING

CHAPTER ONE

TEN REASONS DECISIONS GO WRONG

ABOUT FOUR YEARS AGO, DAMON'S COMPANY, LEARNIT, decided to bring on a Chief Operating Officer (COO).

Damon had been CEO for twenty-plus years at that time.[3] Most of his day was taken up wrangling details. This is a problem all too familiar for small business owners. Working in the business takes up so much time that you can't work *on the business.* Learnit had hit a certain threshold, and it could go no further without a change.

It felt to Damon like a COO might be the solution. He pictured a trusted right-hand person, his second in command, who could be excellent at the day-to-day. He imagined a person who would observe what Learnit had in place, and then use their experience to evolve the operations and team for the better. Most of all, he pictured getting more of his day back.

---

3   To prevent confusion, we've chosen to tell stories involving Damon's or Kandis's personal experiences using our individual names. Even so, rest assured that each story comes straight from the source!

Hiring at that level would be a big investment for Learnit and a big risk. If it took Damon out of firefighting and created opportunities for other earnings and investments, though, it would be worth it. Damon dreamed of having the time to anticipate customers' future needs, or even consider that subscription model he'd been eying for years.

It seemed like the perfect plan.

Learnit got a job description together, and resumes came pouring in. One stuck out. The applicant had gone to an Ivy League school and had run the learning and development team at a major tech company. She hit all the right points in the interview. She seemed absolutely perfect.

Damon will be the first to admit that he has been known, once or twice, to rush into decisions. He's enthusiastic by nature, he likes to check tasks off his list, and occasionally he'll skip a step to get there. After the interview with this "perfect" candidate, Damon got excited. He stopped looking at other applicants, and when the other interviewers brought up red flags, he ignored them. He didn't consider the long-term risks of handing his beloved company over to a stranger. Instead of doing a contract-to-hire or other risk-mitigation strategy, he made up his mind that this was the way the company was going to go. She was the person. He didn't even consult everyone on the executive team.

The new COO was a terrible fit. (Did you guess this is where we were going?) She made sweeping changes without bothering to study the systems already in place. She tried to run the forty-person team like a large organization. She dictated rather than persuaded. She sat in her office and told others what to do, rather than rolling up her sleeves to actively work beside the team.

This style of management fundamentally didn't work for

the small consensus-based culture of Learnit. Her decisions alienated the team and led to massive chaos, anxiety, and destruction. A key team member on the operations team left, and others were threatened. Productivity plummeted.

At no point was Damon freed up. If anything, the disruptions led to more hands-on time than before, at a much higher stress load. He was constantly fielding emails from people under her, and meeting with customers to repair relationships broken by fast-changing policies. The whole experience was frustrating and emotionally painful. Damon lost weeks of sleep.

After three months, he and the new COO mutually agreed the job was not for her, and she moved on.

Damon stood in front of his team and apologized. What had happened was on him. The hire was his mistake, and he thanked every person on the team for sticking it out so long. He invited them to join him in his humble walk back to the drawing board. Learnit would learn from the experience, and he wanted their input on exactly how they should.

HINDSIGHT IS 20/20

How did this bad decision happen? Damon let his excitement blind him. He rushed to the answer rather than slowing down to consider the options or listen to the team. He wanted the outcome too much.

This was a high-stakes decision, and they had the luxury of time. Damon could have listened to his team when they spotted red flags. He could have explored the culture fit more carefully. They could have vetted and interviewed more candidates.

In retrospect, he also should have thought through long-term risks. They had never hired someone in this position before. What would be the impact on team members? Would new policies damage relationships with long-standing clients? What would really happen with Damon's workload? Damon didn't consider any of the worst-case scenarios until they arrived. If he had, perhaps the harm could have been at least partially mitigated.

Considering the high stakes, Learnit (and Damon) needed a better decision-making *process* than what they used. Beginning in Chapter Four, we'll share our own, strong decision-making process. First, though, we'll need to talk about the common mistakes that can lead to bad decisions.

What are the most common decision mistakes, and how can you avoid making them?

1. RUSHING THE DECISION

Our first common mistake in decision-making is rushing. Deciding out of artificial urgency or a knee-jerk reaction is asking for trouble. So is rushing out of emotion, even positive emotions, like enthusiasm. Rushing is a problem, no matter the reason.

If a salesperson pushes artificial urgency, you might say yes. *You'll get an extra month of service if you act now. Yes!* Later, you regret having been swayed. Turns out neither the timing nor the cost was right for you.

Sometimes you find yourself saying yes before thinking through all the impacts. Say you're someone who travels for work. We see so many professionals who are overcommitted, but none more so than business travelers. Often they forget to factor in all the time, costs, and delays before agreeing to yet another cross-country commitment. Especially now, in 2023, as we're coming out of the global pandemic. People are itching to get off the ground again but may find themselves juggling time zones and hotels. Stretched thin and physically exhausted. That kind of fatigue isn't sustainable in the long term.

Similarly, an impulse decision on New Year's might lead you to purchase a treadmill and hundreds of dollars in online classes. Six months later, the only use you've gotten out of the treadmill is as a clothes rack in your studio apartment. You did not watch a single class. Rushing the decision in the moment meant you wasted money you could have spent on other, more valuable, pursuits.

The solution to rushing is to *slow* down. Think carefully. Is the decision or purchase really necessary? Is there a real-time issue, or is the sense of urgency artificial? Put another way: Do you really have to reply to that email today? What will be lost if you instead reply tomorrow, when you can give it more thoughtful attention?

Stop saying yes without thinking! You'd be surprised at how few people will get upset when you tell them no. Not long ago, Damon was asked by the CEO of a startup to join the company's Advisory Board. He was honored, but he understood the kind of time commitment involved. He looked at what he had on his plate—growth at Learnit, a second kid on the way—and knew he didn't have the bandwidth. Damon expressed his gratitude, and then his regret, and the CEO—instead of getting mad, thanked Damon. He appreciated his candor. The board position was important to him too, obviously, and he didn't want someone saying yes just for the sake of yes. He needed a fully committed board member. It's always nerve-racking to say no. But a "no" upfront is better than a "whoops" down the line.

2. GETTING STUCK IN ANALYSIS PARALYSIS

Damon and Kandis will tell you that in the past they have tended to rush decisions. Not everyone rushes. Some people have a different problem: analysis paralysis. This tendency is just as damaging, not because of impulsivity, but because of missed opportunities.

Analysis paralysis is a state of internal paralysis, a feeling of powerlessness or inability to act. When you're stuck in analysis paralysis, you feel you can't decide until you have more information, or until you can do more with the data that you have. You won't ever move forward to making the actual decision.

Analysis paralysis is rooted in anxiety. Oftentimes people are afraid of making a mistake. They want to get it perfect. If you're here, reading a book about decision-making, you might relate. It's hard not to hold on tightly, especially when the choice *matters*. The more important or high stakes the situation, the more often analysis paralysis kicks in. You think if you just get more information, you'll feel better about making a decision. Sadly, this is an illusion. Data is constantly changing, and if the issue is fear, no amount of information will make you feel perfectly settled.

Choosing not to make a decision is still a decision, and usually not a great one. Delays cost opportunities. Recently, Damon and his wife began interviewing nannies to look after their two young children. They met their ideal candidate. She had everything they wanted, had passed all the background checks, and was ready to go...but she was one of the first people they interviewed. They felt they had to do their due diligence and owed it to themselves to interview the other candidates. So they met with all the other potential nannies, and none of them held a candle to their favorite. After five days, they circled back and offered her the job.

It was too late.

In that time, she'd already interviewed for, been offered, and accepted another position. As the old proverb says, you have to "strike while the iron is hot." Opportunities go cold if you don't take advantage of them in a timely manner.

In the real world, you'll never get all the information you want for a perfect decision. Perfect doesn't exist. If you've done your due diligence, trust that you have enough. Take a step back, look at the big picture and what you know, and make the decision. By all means, document why you made the decision and your assumptions in making it so that you can revisit the issue as the situation changes. Be certain that you know *why* you are making the decision in the first place, and be reasonably sure that your decision addresses the intent. However, don't obsess over the details to the point of inaction.

Having a solid process, like the one in Part Two of this book, can be very helpful in focusing you when you feel stuck in analysis paralysis. Go through the process and act even if you do not feel fully comfortable. Deliberate action is the cure for analysis paralysis. With time and practice, you'll grow more confident in moving forward in difficult situations.

Organizations also have a role to play in decreasing decision anxiety by creating safe environments. When people can learn from mistakes and be empowered to make decisions related to their jobs freely, the stakes get lower, and decisions happen more quickly.

3. FAILING TO DEFINE SUCCESS

"If you don't know where you're going, any road will get you there."

—LOUIS CARROLL

Any road will work if you have no destination in mind—until you're halfway to Kansas and realize you need to be in California. Do you have somewhere you want to get? Define success and the journey becomes radically easier.

With Damon's COO decision, he knew from a high level what success would look like. It would be him spending 20 percent of his time working in the business rather than 80 percent. That was the impact on Damon. However, he didn't do enough extra work to define what actions or approaches the COO would take to make that impact possible.

Oftentimes when leaders hire people and those people struggle on the job, it's because the leader could not articulate what success was supposed to look like; they couldn't define and communicate the future state they wanted. The best team member in the world can't deliver what the leader can't ask for.

In the case of hiring a social media manager, for example, you can make success more likely with good conversations. After you interview a candidate, have them share with you their understanding of what success looks like. Share your own expectations. Describe what a successful future would look like in social media after three months. Have a discussion to bridge the gap between your definition and theirs. The clearer you can make this definition, especially after the hire, the better.

A clear success definition is crucial to translate a good decision into a good outcome. We'll return to how success can be defined and shared in Chapter Four.

4. FAILING TO CONSIDER RISK

Good decision-makers consider consequences and plan for risk. There are several robust risk-assessment models, but before you start making calculations, we'd like you to start with a simple question.

Ask yourself, "What would the worst-case scenario be like in six months to a year?" Then, once you have a deep understanding of the worst case, ask yourself, "Can I live with it?"

Damon did not consider the true worst-case scenario for the COO hire. He thought he'd considered bad effects, but they were all surface level. He'd assumed any bumps in the road could be dealt with quickly and the plan could be back on track with minimal issues. Instead, the outcome of losing loyal employees was very painful, and it took many months to recover.

As you consider your own high-impact decisions, go several layers deeper than might feel necessary. For example, if you're in a relationship and considering moving in together, you will need to consider what happens if the relationship doesn't work out. Who gets the house? Who gets the dog? What if your person lives there for five years—how will you divide the equity?

Many people don't want to think through long-term consequences and risks because, as our examples show, it can be painful. However, it's critical to fully understand if you have the risk tolerance to follow through on the decision. Can you accept the worst-case scenario? Also, consider the risk of *not* taking action or making a decision. Sometimes this risk is worse than making a bad decision!

In March 2023, Silicon Valley Bank (SVB) was taken over by regulators. This was a shock to many. It seems several missteps led to the failure of SVB, and better risk management could have helped them survive. "I think this is a colossal failure in asset-liability risk management," said Mark T. Williams, a former bank examiner for the Federal Reserve.

To provide additional context, SVB offered relatively higher rates on deposits compared with many larger rivals, as many of their clients were venture capital companies. To help fund these higher rates, SVB bought what are often considered "safe" assets, such as US Treasuries and government-backed higher-yielding bonds. However, this was before the Federal Reserve began aggressively hiking rates, starting in 2022. Because of this, the value of most of the bonds SVB purchased declined substantially, as bond values generally decrease as interest rates increase. After SVB announced that it lost $1.8 billion in asset sales, the bank failed to secure additional investment capital and many customers rapidly withdrew deposits, leading to their collapse.[4]

SVB went without a Chief Risk Officer for more than eight months. Maybe having one in place during those critical months in 2022/2023 anticipating what could go wrong and working to mitigate it, could have made a difference.

Don't underestimate the value of risk management.

If you can accept the risks of moving forward, decide confidently. Use data to support your case. If not, take steps to talk through or mitigate the worst case, or choose to walk away. Whatever you decide, be deliberate.

5. GETTING STUCK IN BINARY THINKING

Binary thinking is on or off, yes or no, black or white, this or that. It's easy to get stuck in binary thinking, but there's no

---

4 Sheryl Estrada, "A Risk Management Nightmare at Silicon Valley Bank," *Fortune*, March 13, 2023, https://fortune.com/2023/03/13/risk-management-nightmare-silicon-valley-bank/.

worse ride to be on. Binary thinking hamstrings and clouds judgment. The best answer is usually not one of the two obvious first options.

Stepping out of the quicksand of this kind of thinking just requires a small amount of effort on the front end. Before you get stuck in either/or, find several alternatives that allow you to meet your goal by other means. Brainstorm on your own. Ask others. Think outside the box. When you're given advice or suggestions, get curious rather than defaulting to a knee-jerk *no*. You want to increase your options past two, but not to infinity.

Studies have shown that increasing your options leads to better outcomes—to a point. More options are always better when brainstorming. Even moving from two to three options increases your chance of hitting the right decision by 30 percent! Add in a few more choices, and your odds get even better. In a 2018 article published in the journal *Nature Human Behaviour*, about how "choice overload" affects us (and why it makes deciding to feel so impossible) they found that twelve options are the sweet spot for decision-making.[5] That's enough to excite the brain, without jamming your signal with too many choices. Twelve options feel like a lot, instead of the habitual two, but start with at least a handful and see how far you get.

Later in the book, you'll learn how to create more options in the brainstorming process, and to narrow the options down via prioritization. The wider field prevents binary thinking from taking over, and the narrowing-down process prevents the brain from getting overwhelmed during decision-making.

How could Damon have broken out of binary thinking in his

5   Elena Reutskaja et al., "Choice Overload Reduces Neural Signatures of Choice Set Value in Dorsal Striatum and Anterior Cingulate Cortex," *Nature Human Behaviour* 2 (2018): 925–935, https://doi.org/10.1038/s41562-018-0440-2.

decision? Maybe, instead of hiring his original choice for COO, Damon could have brought in a handful of candidates for secondary interviews. Or, as he explored later, maybe other roles would have accomplished the goal of freeing up his time better. Getting too hung up on that one candidate prevented him from seeing ways to achieve the goal by other means.

Binary thinking limits creativity. Without any pressure to generate alternatives, your binary options will stay black or white. We'll discuss how to harness creativity and brainstorm effective options in Chapter Six.

6. TREATING SYMPTOMS RATHER THAN ROOT CAUSES

There's a famous parable, sometimes attributed to the 1930s community organizer Saul Alinsky, that illustrates how you can easily fall into treating symptoms and not causes.

The parable goes like this:

You're walking past a rushing river. From out of nowhere, a person appears in the current. They are drowning. You leap in to save them. But just as you pull them safely onto shore, another person careens past, also struggling, caught in the current. You leap in again.

You do this over and over, as more and more people float past.

Until finally you have a realization: you're wasting your time pulling people to safety. What you should be doing is running upstream to figure out why all of these people are falling into the river to begin with.

This parable has been shared in business contexts for years. It's popular because it resonates with people. It's so easy for all of us to get caught up, drowning in busy work, treating symptoms without ever taking the time to identify root causes.

The symptoms can feel urgent. Like saving a drowning swimmer. If that's the case, no matter how slow or arduous the task is, we assume it must be the right course of action. It never occurs to us to abandon the swimmers (the symptoms) and go to the mouth of the river (root cause). But to commit to pulling people out of the river is a never-ending process. Your work will suffer because of it.

It's unfortunate, then, that the people who are praised at work are often the ones who put out the fires. They save the day at the last second, and they are rewarded for it. No one rewards the person sitting and thinking about root causes, but they should. Fighting fires may feel good in the moment, but what if you could avoid the fires in the first place?

Symptoms will keep coming until the root cause is dealt with. Peel back the layers and be honest. What, exactly, is the root cause of this issue? How do we solve it, even if solving it is temporarily harder? What needs to break, and what can't break, to solve the real problem?

If you're sick and getting sicker, eventually you'll head to the doctor. They'll give you something to address your symptoms. Tests will be performed. Eventually the illness or disease that's at the heart of your trouble will get addressed, but what if you had been preventative? What if you had committed to healthy habits, regular screening, and stress reduction? Maybe you could have nipped that illness in the bud before it caused you any problems to begin with.

In the same way, if you have a salesperson with a toxic attitude, the right answer for the team might be to let them go. That might feel risky. It may negatively impact the sales numbers for two quarters. Long term, if you take the plunge, you'll be much better off, but you have to be willing to tolerate the short-term pain to succeed.

If, however, you were to only treat the symptoms, you'd quickly find yourself stretched thin. All of that time handling customer complaints, brainstorming incentives to get your outlier on track, and trying to manage coworker morale, would take vital energy away from real business needs.

Treating the root cause is difficult, but it's the only way forward.

7. BEING BLINDED BY BIASES

The human brain uses shortcuts to process information about the world. Sometimes, those shortcuts become biases, and sometimes these biases are harmful. Think of a bias like a blind spot, a gut reaction that is often not true. Some biases are universal to everyone, and some are more specific to individuals. *Psychology Today* defines a bias this way:

"A bias is a tendency, inclination, or prejudice toward or against something or someone. Some biases are positive and helpful—like choosing to only eat foods that are considered healthy or staying away from someone who has knowingly caused harm. But biases are often based on stereotypes, rather than actual knowledge of an individual or circumstance. Whether positive or negative, such cognitive shortcuts can result in prejudgments that lead to rash decisions or discriminatory practices."

Here are four common biases that tend to derail decision-making.

CONFIRMATION BIAS

Confirmation bias is exactly what it sounds like. It is a bias toward confirming your own existing opinions. Say you've been asked to research a topic, one you have strong feelings about. You go out and only collect research that affirms what you already think. You find people and sources to agree with you. Instead of going into an issue with an open mind, seeking to learn, you choose to shore up your existing worldview. That is confirmation bias.

You don't even have to be *consciously* seeking to confirm your opinion for this bias to exist. In fact, it's most dangerous when you're doing it by accident.

Confirmation bias is particularly dangerous for leaders. If you surround yourself only with people who agree with you, and your opinions, you might run the whole organization off a cliff and no one will say a word until you're already broken at the bottom.

Avoid confirmation bias by giving a seat at the decision-making table to individuals with diverse opinions who aren't afraid to challenge the status quo. Hire for diversity of experience and backgrounds—and listen to people when they speak. (It's worth noting that empowering your team to speak up— making them feel they are in the game, and not just filling the bench—is the *inclusion* part of diversity and inclusion. We'll just touch on it here, but there are many excellent books on the subject that we suggest seeking out, if this is a topic that's of interest to you. Search on the internet for "DEIB" and you can make your selection.)

An atmosphere of diversity and inclusion can radically de-risk your decision-making. Confirmation bias is costly. Do the legwork to avoid it before there are high-impact decisions on the line.

THE SUNK COST FALLACY

The Sunk Cost Fallacy is the tendency to continue to invest in a situation because you've already put so much into it. When a company keeps pouring money into an already-failed initiative, refusing to kill it for fear all of those resources will be "wasted," that's the sunk cost fallacy. It's too painful to consider losing what has already been spent, so you continue to throw money or time toward a project that has a slim to no chance of being successful.

In 2013, the Air Force reviewed its Expeditionary Combat Support System (ECSS), a program that began in 2004, and came to the conclusion that over $1 billion had been wasted without yielding "any significant military capability." This outcome wasn't a surprise. The program, which had been a massive undertaking, was aimed at modernizing the service's global supply chain.

The goal was to replace outdated Air Force computer systems with a single integrated enterprise resource planning (ERP) system. The software would provide an end-to-end logistics transformation, replacing more than 420 aging systems and serving 250,000 end users across the country. After eight years, the program was canceled without ever going live.

Twice the project was restructured from the ground up, once in 2009 and again in 2011. It was going badly, and people knew the technical aspects and execution would not work as planned. They tried to break the project up into smaller, more manageable-size efforts. Unfortunately, even after the first restructure, the decision was made to keep pouring resources into the project, even though progress had come to a standstill. Eventually they were forced to pull the plug.

All along there were signs that the program wasn't working, but leaders refused to call it quits. Unrealistic performance expectations, poor management, and a lack of decisiveness all exacerbated the already failing undertaking. A letter sent to the Under Secretary of Defense in 2013 put it this way:

> The full motivation of decision-makers at these points is difficult to reconstruct now—over-optimism, a preference for the status quo, and justifying program continuation based on accrued sunk costs all seem to have played a part...[6]

Had someone in a position of leadership been willing to sacrifice the money already spent and pull the plug earlier, that $1 billion/eight-year number might have been significantly smaller.

Stay open and humble. Make a decision, and then, when the facts change, change the decision. Be vulnerable enough and honest enough to admit to failure, at least to yourself. Stop the loss. Then, pivot. You'll be spending your extra cash on valuable priorities, while the other players are doubling down on strategies that are already proven not to work.

Leaders often understand the money part of this bias, but seeing how time or resources can be sunk costs is more challenging. Take for example, the story of Bob Chapek and the Walt Disney Company. Chapek was the successor for Disney's former (and long-running) CEO, Bob Iger. After two years of poor earnings and political upheaval under Chapek, the Board of Directors at Disney made a strategic decision. Even though Chapek still had years on his contract, they decided it was worth more to oust him and reinstate Bob Iger, than to watch the company continue to struggle.

---

6   Gary R. Bliss to Under Secretary of Defense for Acquisition and Sustainment, "Root Cause Analysis of the Expeditionary Combat Support System Program," August 28, 2013, Department of Defense, https://www.acq.osd.mil/asda/ae/ada/docs/2013-08-28-parca-rca-ecss.pdf.

Iger quickly took action in making organizational changes. He reversed some of the poor decisions that Chapek had made, putting decision-making in the wrong hands and generally muddying the waters when it came to the breakdown of decision-making roles. According to a memo Iger sent to employees upon his return, he tasked top execs with building a "new structure that puts more decision-making back in the hands of our creative teams and rationalizes costs."[7]

Had they allowed themselves to fall victim to the sunk cost fallacy, they may have assumed they were "stuck" with Chapek. Instead, they took the financial hit by continuing to pay Chapek what was left on his contract, and made a call they felt would benefit the organization in the long run.

You won't get your original resources back by doubling down. Cut your losses, and move on.

If you can, use the opportunity to learn. Go back to the original decision and figure out if you need to take alternate action in the future. Mistakes are expensive, but the expense pays off in learning.

THE AVAILABILITY HEURISTIC

People are also biased toward circumstances they can more easily remember. The availability heuristic is a mental shortcut that people use to estimate the likelihood of an event based on how easily they can bring examples of similar events to mind. Essentially, people tend to overestimate the probability of events that are more easily recalled or readily available in their memory,

---

7   Drew Taylor, "Read Bob Iger's First Message to Disney Employees as Reinstated CEO," Yahoo! Entertainment, November 20, 2022, https://www.yahoo.com/entertainment/read-bob-iger-first-message-041246933.html.

regardless of whether those events are actually more common or probable. If you can recall an event easily because it was vivid, emotional, or recent, you will judge that *kind* of event to be more common than others that you do not remember as quickly.

When you are trying to make a decision, a number of related events or situations might immediately spring to the forefront of your thoughts. As a result, you might judge that those events are more frequent or probable than others. You give greater credence to this information and tend to overestimate the probability and likelihood of similar things happening in the future.

Some examples of the Availability Heuristic in action:

Another high-profile violent crime has taken place, the news outlets pick it up, and before you know it, everyone is talking about it. You question your and your family's safety. It feels like crime rates are skyrocketing. In fact, according to a 2022 Pew Research Center article on violent crime and the midterm elections, violent crime rates in the US have held steady, and are well below those seen in the 1990s.[8]

You assume that the job of a police officer is the most dangerous occupation in the United States due to news coverage. You hear about police violence and deaths on the job more often, so it's clearly the more deadly occupation. Right? Wrong. According to the Bureau of Labor Statistics "Census of Fatal Occupational Injuries," *logging* is the most dangerous occupation, ranking thirty-three times more dangerous than the average job, nationwide.[9]

8   John Gramlich, "Violent Crime Is a Key Midterm Voting Issue, but What Does the Data Say?"
    Pew Research Center, October 31, 2022, https://www.pewresearch.org/short-reads/2022/10/31/
    violent-crime-is-a-key-midterm-voting-issue-but-what-does-the-data-say/.

9   U.S. Bureau of Labor Statistics, "Civilian Occupations with High Fatal Work Injury Rates,"
    December 16, 2022, https://www.bls.gov/charts/census-of-fatal-occupational-injuries/civilian-
    occupations-with-high-fatal-work-injury-rates.htm.

So far in 2023, layoffs have cost tens of thousands of tech workers their jobs in the United States. Big names such as Google, Amazon, Microsoft, and Meta have announced cuts. In the context of layoffs, availability bias might lead people to believe that layoffs are more common and likely to happen than they are, simply because they can easily recall instances where they or someone they know was laid off. This can result in people being overly cautious and fearful of losing their jobs, even if the likelihood of a layoff is low. For example, maybe you are a Nurse Practitioner and are stressed about the possibility of layoffs, even though employment of nurse anesthetists, nurse midwives, and nurse practitioners is projected to grow 40 percent from 2021 to 2031.[10] The chances of layoffs for people with your skillset are unlikely.

As for leaders making staffing decisions for their organization, it is also important to be mindful of this bias. One Stanford Professor argues that many of the layoffs in the tech industry may be from copycat or imitation behavior.[11] If you are working for a tech company and look around and see many other companies in your industry laying people off, it may lead you to think that your company will be next or should be next. Take extra steps to do your homework and not be basing judgments and decisions on information just because it is easily available (i.e., top news story for this week).

---

10   US Bureau of Labor Statistics, "Nurse Anesthetists, Nurse Midwives, and Nurse Practitioners," in *Occupational Outlook Handbook*, last modified September 8, 2022, https://www.bls.gov/ooh/healthcare/nurse-anesthetists-nurse-midwives-and-nurse-practitioners.htm.

11   Sarah Jackson, "I'm a Stanford Professor Who's Studied Organizational Behavior for Decades. The Widespread Layoffs in Tech Are More Because of Copycat Behavior than Necessary Cost-Cutting," *Insider*, March 25, 2023, https://www.businessinsider.com/stanford-professor-mass-layoffs-caused-by-social-contagion-companies-imitating-2023-2?r=US&IR=T.

THE ANCHORING BIAS

Anchoring bias is a cognitive bias in which people rely too heavily on the first piece of information they receive when making subsequent judgments or decisions. In his book, *Predictably Irresistible,* Dan Ariely posits that the best way to reassure a customer about a very high price tag is to anchor expectations first. For example, we'd suggest saying, "Don't worry. This isn't a $50,000 proposal." That's your anchor. You have no intention of charging them $50,000 but it's where you'd like them to put their baseline. That way, when you show them your $10,000 proposal, they will feel relieved—like they're getting a deal. Your anchor makes $10K feel like a pittance.

If you're a salesperson, the anchoring bias is your friend. If you're making decisions, especially with a salesperson across the table from you, you don't want to fall for that kind of anchoring.

In the case of the $10,000 proposal, don't depend on the number that the salesperson gives you. Instead, do your research on costs. If everyone else is charging $2,000 for the same service, your $10,000 proposal is overpriced regardless of the anchor.

The same is true for salary at a new job. You should always ignore the initial number and ask for what you expect due to what the market is paying for your skillset.[12]

Anchoring also relates to events. For example, if a news report on a winter storm predicts it will be a blizzard with twelve feet of snow, people could anchor their perception of the severity of the event on that prediction. As new informa-

---

12 Mighty Knowledge, "Anchoring Bias: How to Avoid Getting Ripped Off on Salary," *ILLUMINATION,* Medium, August 19, 2020, https://medium.com/illumination/anchoring-bias-how-to-avoid-getting-ripped-off-on-salary-43977293cf76.

tion becomes available that suggests the storm may actually be much weaker, bringing inches of snow versus feet, people may still perceive it as a very dangerous event because their initial anchor was so extreme, making decisions accordingly.

Anchoring bias can be a powerful influence on how people perceive and respond to events, and can lead to errors in judgment and decision-making.

8. MAKING DECISIONS IN A SILO

Good decisions require communication—an exchange of information. Simply put, you need to talk. Specifically, you need to talk with other stakeholders affected by the decision. There's no shortcut.

The more high stakes the decision, the more critical it is to ask for input from other people. The executive team had insights into the COO candidate that Damon needed. So did the operations team who would be working with the candidate every day.

After the COO moved on to another company, Damon sat down with his executive team to hire another person for the role. He would be making the final hiring decision, but he needed their input. What could they do better this time? Together, the team drafted a persona. They went through a formal interviewing process with a decision matrix (see Chapter Seven). They sought personality tests and looked for culture fit. They had many conversations among the team.

In the end, Damon hired not a COO, but a VP of Product and Customer Experience. They started on a ninety-day contract. Expectations were clear: no major organizational changes would be made during the contract. Instead, they were asked to use the time to create a roadmap of where they wanted Learnit to go.

The second round decision was successful. The person has been with Learnit for three years now and they are doing an amazing job. Damon is freed up to work on strategic projects, and the company is growing steadily. His expectations are more realistic now, and the input from the stakeholders and the team affected has been priceless.

Good decision-making means knowing what you are promising. If there will be secondary effects, you should know what those are too. This requires conversations with all your stakeholders, including the people most affected by the change.

Skip these conversations at your peril.

9. ALLOWING AMBIGUITY IN DECISION ROLES

Ambiguity about decision-making roles will stoke the fires of resentment. Make expectations clear and have conversations with the people who will be directly affected by your decision. If the team believes that they will be voting on the decision, and instead the leader is making it unilaterally, chaos will ensue.

Too often people are asked to provide a recommendation regarding a decision and assume their recommendation is what will be implemented. Setting clear expectations will solve this problem entirely.

Consider saying:

Decision-Maker (before the decision): "We have an important decision ahead of us. I would appreciate everyone's input, and at the end of the day, I will be making the final decision."

Decision-Maker (after the decision): "I carefully considered all of your valuable input, and here is why I made the decision I did... I now expect everyone to get on board and support the decision."

Ambiguity leads to conflict and lowers morale. It can also damage the execution of the decision, which leads to the decision ultimately being unsuccessful. Clarity takes effort to establish but makes all the elements of the decision go more smoothly.

We'll discuss establishing decision-making roles and setting clear expectations in Chapter Three.

10. IMPLEMENTING POORLY

There can be a lot of discord leading up to making a high-impact decision. All of the prep and stress take its toll. Because of this, it's easy to confuse "making the decision" with the goal itself. Stakeholders go into a meeting room, have hours of challenging conversations, make the decision...and assume they're done. This is a mistake. Sadly, the end state does not rain magically from the sky. You cannot buy a house without inspections and mortgage qualifications, no matter which house you pick. Choosing a technology platform for the company doesn't install it or train the team members who will be using it. The real success or failure of a decision often happens in implementation.

Perhaps it's natural to take your foot off the gas once the decision has been made. You've done all the groundwork. You've investigated, done due diligence, and worked very hard to find the right direction. You're proud of yourself (and rightly so) for the decision you made. The hard part feels like it's over.

The hardest work is not the decision; the hardest work is following through.

We'll return to implementation and how to ensure it goes well in Chapter Ten and Chapter Eleven.

WHAT'S NEXT?

Here, we've covered Ten Reasons Decisions Go Wrong so that you can spot them in your own decision processes. By avoiding them, you will immediately see more success.

Of course, avoiding the traps isn't as easy as it sounds. If it was, we could end the book right here. Rushing through a decision out of emotion is satisfying. Confirmation bias can be sneaky, and we all fall prey to binary thinking now and again.

People make thousands of decisions every day. No one can avoid every pothole. No matter how careful you are, no matter how carefully you approach decision processes and tools, you will inevitably make bad decisions. The numbers game makes it inevitable. So don't get down on yourself when you do. Instead, learn from your mistakes. It's key to decision-making...and to life.

One of the best ways to learn from your mistakes is by thinking about how you think and focusing on the mindset of good decision-making. Read on to find out how.

CHAPTER TWO

THE PSYCHOLOGY OF DECISION MAKING

MAKING DECISIONS FROM YOUR GUT FEELS NATURAL. Excitement or fear can feel like good reasons to make decisions fast. Unfortunately, gut feelings and emotions are usually poor deciders. They lead you to jump to conclusions. They lead you to decide without regard to risks or other options. Under the grip of emotion, you don't see the future impact of your actions.

A much better course of action is to decide from rational thought. Logic is the domain of the brain, so let's start there.

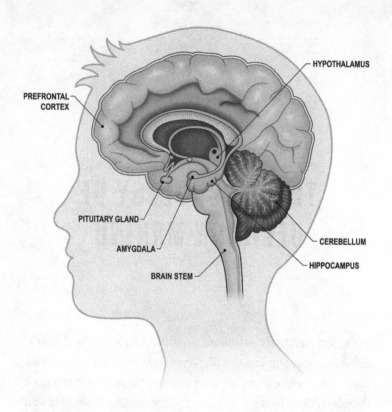

The prefrontal cortex (an area of the frontal lobe) is the part of the brain located behind our forehead. It's responsible for executive functions, memory, attention, and emotional regulation. Executive function includes decision-making, specifically the kind of decision-making that's rational rather than impulsive. The prefrontal cortex is good at spotting patterns and connecting ideas with probable consequences. It can think five steps ahead.

The limbic system is a set of brain structures that include the hippocampus and amygdala. This is the part of the brain that controls our emotions, our sense of time, long-term memory, and emotional behavior. If you act without thinking, it likely involves the limbic system. The amygdala ties emotional meanings to our memories, and it controls the fight or flight response. If we react immediately to fear or anger, the amygdala will wrest control of our decision-making at that moment. The amygdala also runs what's called the reward and punishment processing center, where the brain connects emotional impulses to immediate rewards and punishments.

The limbic system plays a key role in how animals assess and respond to environmental threats and challenges. It's the center of instinct, where animals avoid punishment and seek out rewards or go into fight-or-flight responses. This part of the brain is fantastic if you need to run from an immediate threat. It's also great if you need to make a fast decision to get an immediate, tangible, concrete reward, like money or a slice of cake. There are absolutely times when emotional impulsive decisions are the right answer, and the limbic system handles these emergencies well. It will keep you alive.

Making long-term, high-impact decisions from the limbic system, on the other hand, is troublesome. When you send an email you regret or agree to buy a product you don't need on impulse, your limbic brain is in charge. In some cases, these impulses can have long-term, negative consequences. The limbic system has no consideration other than for what feels good at the moment.

The more rational prefrontal cortex is capable of considering consequences and making sustainable, long-term plans that include many competing factors. Decisions that have real consequences *must* be made with the prefrontal cortex for the best outcomes to occur. However, the limbic system is "louder" and will override your prefrontal cortex if allowed to. That's why it's important to make decisions from logic and consideration rather than from impulse. Give your prefrontal cortex a chance to kick in and consider all of the factors.

IMPULSIVITY AND THE BRAIN

Margot goes to a restaurant that's short-staffed. She waits to be seated, and after ordering and waiting for twenty minutes at the table, her food still hasn't come. In reality, her food will be up next. Instead of asking the server about when her food will be ready, she stands up and throws her napkin on the table. She walks out of the restaurant rather than wait the additional five minutes for her food. Now she has to wait in line for another forty minutes at the next restaurant, which makes no logical sense. Yet, her frustration at not getting what she wanted in the time she wanted it overruled her logic. We have all been there!

We all understand the difficulties of making decisions out of emotion when it comes to our personal lives. Impulse control in our work lives is often even harder to spot and manage.

FORMAL DECISION-MAKING AS A CURE FOR FIREFIGHTING

Everyone is time bankrupt these days. You start the day with more on your to-do list than you could possibly get done, and the pile just grows. Decisions about priorities become constant, to the point of decision fatigue. When Mark Zuckerberg was asked about wearing the same color shirt every day at work, he responded he didn't want to make decisions about frivolous tasks.[13] He wanted to eliminate smaller decisions so that he could focus on higher-impact ones. He wanted to save his decision-making energy for the critical ones. Barack Obama has a similar mono-wardrobe. So did Einstein.

---

13   Kathleen Elkins, "Billionaires Mark Zuckerberg and John Paul DeJoria Use a Simple Wardrobe Trick to Boost Productivity," Make It, CNBC, January 5, 2017, https://www.cnbc.com/2017/01/05/mark-zuckerberg-and-john-paul-dejorias-simple-wardrobe-trick.html.

Considered decision-making is controlled by the executive function of the brain, and like a muscle, the decision-making function tires over time. When you spend most of your time on busy work and reacting to the latest crisis, it's hard to make time to think through choices that really matter. It's easier to make decisions on emotions and impulses because the feeling of urgency and pressure activates your limbic system. Thinking deeply can feel overwhelming and exhausting.

Yet, decisions made from impulse and emotion rarely turn out well. There are always second-order effects that you haven't thought about. If you buy an IT system for the workplace that won't integrate with another critical system, no matter how flashy and exciting the interface is, you'll have wasted time and money. Making high-impact decisions from the limbic system inevitably leads to unintended consequences.

Make formal thinking, and decision-making, a priority. Challenge yourself to think about a problem or a decision all the way through, from soup to nuts. Yes, that means time, effort, and serious focus. Schedule time to do this deep thinking. We recommend early in the morning, if possible when your brain is fresh. Regardless of when be sure to block time and work through the steps in Part Two of this book strategically and thoughtfully. Otherwise, you will never stop being reactive.

If you know your processes and procedures are broken but don't make time to slow down and fix them, the problem will never get better! If you redesign the processes you'll be more effective, efficient, and far less stressed. Most critical decision-making is like this. Yes, you most likely feel like you can't afford the time on your calendar to think through the decision at length. Schedule it anyway, as an investment.

Employers don't hire leaders or even senior contributors for their ability to do busy work. They hire them for their brains.

In fact, leaders are often hired specifically for their decision-making capabilities. Any time invested in thinking through decisions critically, then, has an immense bang for your buck. The difficulty and emotional overwhelm are part of the investment, and skipping it doesn't do you or anyone else any favors.

Going through a process to make a difficult decision or to solve a significant challenge is hard. In fact, in a study of more than 2,700 leaders, 57 percent of newly appointed executives said that decisions were more complicated and difficult than expected.[14] It's still absolutely worth prioritizing the process. Otherwise, you will make hurried, haphazard decisions you will live to regret.

LIMITING DECISION FATIGUE

One of the most important ways to make better decisions is to make some changes to your day to limit decision fatigue, and to use the decision-making capability you have more strategically.

Decision fatigue is just what it sounds like. It's the weariness that sets in after making too many decisions over a short period of time. Decision fatigue can have a detrimental effect on a person's ability to make additional decisions. So if you're in a leadership position, expected to make decisions quickly and often, decision fatigue is something you should know how to combat.

No matter how confident you are in your ability to make thoughtful decisions, we all have our limits. If you've got a full day, chances are your decision-making powers will be stronger

---

14   Ron Carucci, "Leaders, Stop Avoiding Hard Decisions," *Harvard Business Review*, April 13, 2018, https://hbr.org/2018/04/leaders-stop-avoiding-hard-decisions.

earlier in your workday than later. There are simple steps you can take to set yourself up for success.

DELEGATE

Know which decisions are such that you need to be the one with your hand on the buzzer, and which can be delegated to less senior-level employees. If you can take a decision off your plate, do it.

Remember how Zuckerberg wears uniform-style clothes every day? Since executive function tires like a muscle, it's important to make strategic choices about which decisions *not* to make.

AS JEFF BEZOS SAYS, "AS A SENIOR EXECUTIVE, YOU GET PAID TO MAKE A SMALL NUMBER OF HIGH-QUALITY DECISIONS. YOUR JOB IS NOT TO MAKE THOUSANDS OF DECISIONS EVERY DAY."

Be strategic, and take tasks off your plate, whether by eliminating or delegating.

In your job, which decisions do you personally need to make? Focus on decisions that will make a large impact on your organization, and block time to think them all the way through. That's what you're ultimately getting paid to do. For all of the smaller decisions, work on empowering your team to make them with confidence.

Whether you're very senior or just starting out, it's always better to spend the brain power of your prefrontal cortex making fewer high-impact decisions than making many reactive firefighting decisions. This will not happen naturally; you will have to set yourself up for success strategically.

MANAGE YOUR TIME AND ENERGY

Schedule critical meetings earlier in the day. Even if you're not a morning person, you'll have higher reserves of energy first thing in your day, and will be able to approach high-impact decisions with the focus they deserve. Then, block out time to think through the most critical problems and decisions in the morning, before decision fatigue has a chance to set in.

Outside of work, try to minimize the number of decisions that you make in your life. Perhaps that's handling meal planning and shopping entirely on Sunday afternoons or laying out your outfits for the week in advance. Perhaps that's outsourcing some of your decisions to other people. Whatever you can do to free up your brain to focus on high-impact decisions is well worth doing.

LESS CONTEXT SWITCHING

Most people juggle multiple projects in a day. It takes uninterrupted time devoted to a task to get into a truly productive flow state. According to a 2021 joint report on digital task switching by Qatalog and Cornell University's Ellis Idea Lab, it takes people an average of nine and a half minutes to get back into a productive workflow after switching tasks.[15]

If you are switching tasks dozens (or even hundreds) of times per day, imagine how much time is being wasted just settling back into a state of focus?

Every time you check an email, and then go on to the next task, you are context switching. Every time you're working on

---

15 Language.work and Ellis Idea Lab, *Workgeist Report '21: Research into Culture, Mindset and Productivity for the Modern Work Era* (Qatalog, 2021), 11, https://assets.qatalog.com/language. work/qatalog-2021-workgeist-report.pdf.

Excel and someone drops by your office to interrupt you, you are context switching. All day, every day, we are making decisions about what to prioritize and what to return to. It makes our heads hurt, just thinking about it.

As an antidote, plan your day thoughtfully. Run your day so that it doesn't run you. Practice "time blocking" so that you're doing the same task for a prolonged period of time rather than jumping in and out. Set expectations accordingly. Make solid time to think and run through potential decisions, ideally in the morning when you're fresh. No one will make the best decisions at 5:00 p.m. after a work day in which you've context switched three hundred times.

Incidentally, there's been extensive conversation around the maker versus manager schedule (search "maker vs. manager schedule" on your favorite search engine). You can get more out of yourself *and* your people by limiting task-switching demands. Every time someone is interrupted from a mentally taxing task, they lose from twenty minutes to an hour getting back on track. They may even have to start over. So, it's important to be mindful of controlling interruptions for both yourself and for others working with you. It may also be helpful to mutually agree to take on the most challenging task early in the day, and to save collaboration tasks until later.

POWER NAPS

A coffee nap (or caffeine nap) is a strategy for boosting alertness and productivity that involves consuming caffeine and then taking a short nap. The idea is that the caffeine takes about twenty to thirty minutes to take effect, so if you drink a cup of coffee or other caffeinated beverage and then take a nap for roughly twenty minutes, you can wake up feeling more alert and refreshed than if you had just taken a nap or consumed caffeine alone, which means you will have the ability to make better decisions. While coffee naps can be an effective way to boost alertness, we recognize that taking one may not be possible for everyone based on work schedules. However, if you can sneak in a few minutes in the afternoon to take a nap, we highly recommend it. Just be aware that taking one too late in the day may interfere with your sleep![16]

PERSONALITY TYPES

You can think about your personality type like having a favorite room in your house. Everyone has their favorite room, the one they just feel at ease in. If someone spends most of their time in the living room, that doesn't mean they don't get up and go to the kitchen, or do laundry, when the situation calls for it. The living room is simply where they prefer to spend their time.

It's the same with natural personality styles. Research shows that people *can* force themselves to think and behave using other styles. They just prefer their own. To give you an example: Kandis knows, from her own personality type testing, that she will always consider data and details before people and emotions. Yet, because she knows this about herself, and the importance of getting buy-in from stakeholders, she does a sanity check before making any major decision. How is this decision going to make people feel? How should this be communicated in a way that can get people on board? It is often referred to as "flexing" when stepping out of your personality style and employing behaviors less natural to you.

---

16   Jay Summer, "Coffee Nap," Sleep Foundation, last updated February 23, 2023, https://www.sleepfoundation.org/sleep-hygiene/coffee-nap.

Other personality types might instinctively consider people and feelings, but struggle with data and details. Those people will tend toward emotional decisions and unintended consequences. Someone with Kandis's inclinations, but without self-awareness could tend toward factual decisions that make everyone around them upset. As long as you think through the opposite of your tendency, then, neither personality is better than the other. They both have strengths and weaknesses. It can also be helpful to involve people with different personality types when making a high-impact decision, to ensure you consider different perspectives. This is the value of having differences on your team, regarding how people think.

Everyone has a natural personality and a natural style for decision-making. Each is equally important and valuable, and each contains its own strengths and blind spots. The personality test is not what is important; no one will match a given test perfectly, as inborn preferences and experiences make up the results, and there are dozens of tests available to choose from. What is important is the opportunity to know yourself.

PERSONALITY TESTS

Much of the information about personality types builds upon research from the late 1800s and the early 1900s. This same research as it's evolved over the years informs multiple tests. Each test has value as it tries to describe the complexity of peoples' personalities. Each test also has its limitations.

In 1921, Swiss psychologist Carl G. Jung wrote *Psychological Type*. It was one of the books about inborn preferences and personality types. The book eventually made its way to America, where two women, Isabel Briggs-Myers and her mother Catherine Cook, developed Jung's ideas into a formal test to reliably separate people into personality types, known as Myers-Briggs Type Indicator® (MBTI®). They believed that helping people better understand others could lead to less conflict in the world.

The DiSC model is also a popular personality test, based on the work of psychologist William Moulton Marston in the 1920s. The DiSC typing system is a popular, straightforward, standardized, and relatively easy way to assess behavioral styles and preferences.

No matter which test you use, or whether you decide to skip formal testing altogether—it's worth taking a closer look at your own personality and tendencies. Knowledge is power. If you know where you habitually lean, you'll understand how to apply the necessary counterbalance, as well as what kinds of people to surround yourself with when a high-impact decision is at stake.

THE DISC ASSESSMENT

The DiSC assessment is our go-to for personality testing.[17] It's simple and we find it more user-friendly than some of the others. To use DiSC to determine your personality type, you take a forced-choice assessment that takes approximately twenty minutes of your time. Assessment results are based on your life experiences and natural style (personality).

The assessment results for DiSC focus on four main quadrants:

D for dominance,

i for influence,

S for steadiness, and

C for conscientiousness.

---

17 https://www.everythingdisc.com/.

Each quadrant represents key characteristics. All DiSC styles are valuable and important to have represented on a team; one is not better than another! The i's and the S's tend to be more accepting and warm, and the D's and C's tend to be more questioning and skeptical. The D's and i's tend to be more fast-paced and outspoken, and the C's and S's tend to be more cautious and reflective.

D FOR DOMINANCE

Dominant people tend to lean toward extroversion and take action quickly. Their number one focus is results.

Sometimes this personality type moves too quickly for other people's taste. Their plans are not always well-thought-out. They can get in trouble by missing details.

I FOR INFLUENCE

They bring incredible enthusiasm to the table and are good with relationships. Big-picture thinking comes easily to them. They also tend to move quickly and may miss the details when it comes to executing.

S FOR STEADINESS

The steadiness group loves to provide support and are sometimes referred to as our peacekeepers. They keep other people top of mind, and they don't like to ruffle feathers. The S type wants to get everyone else on board. They will lean into consensus and collaboration all day long, which can slow down the process.

C FOR CONSCIENTIOUSNESS

Conscientious people value accuracy above all. They are detail-oriented and excellent at risk management. As a result, they tend to move more slowly.

Sometimes, C types come across to others as more cynical or negative, always poking holes in the plan. Since they want to ensure they've got all the pieces perfectly in place, they can end up in analysis paralysis.

BUILDING A WELL-ROUNDED TEAM

All four quadrants have strengths and blind spots, each with its own communication style. The best teams tend to be made up of a well-rounded group of people, with different styles balancing each other out.

The same is true for decision-making. When making a decision, it's important to "leave your favorite room" and consider the view from elsewhere. Pretend you're another personality type altogether. Does the landscape look different? Are certain options more or less appealing? Get someone who identifies as another type to help you talk through your decision. Collaborating and brainstorming with others will broaden your perspective in a way that is extremely helpful for high-impact decisions.

Don't make a critical decision in a silo—lost in your own thoughts. Involve other people and other styles. Some will lean toward data, and others will consider the people and emotions. Some will move quickly and may miss details. Others will move slowly and get stuck in the minutia. Together, a variety of styles will harmonize, and when it comes to big decisions...the better the "music," the better the outcome.

To get the most out of collaboration with other people, be

aware of what their style is, whether it's Myers-Briggs, DiSC, or an alternative. Then adjust. See where you can be flexible and bend to their viewpoint. Your favorite room is the living room. If your coworker's favorite room is the kitchen, don't yell at them from the living room—*why aren't you in here? It's so much better over here!* Walk over to the kitchen and have a cup of coffee with them. Admire the scenery. Relish being somewhere new. Tailor your style to their needs. When you know how to step out of your natural style and into someone else's, the collaboration gets exponentially more effective.

All types have strengths and weaknesses, and the best work happens when different styles work together. Of course, personality type is not the only aspect of ourselves we will need to be aware of. We will continue to reference personality styles throughout this book, providing suggestions on how to obtain the best outcomes.

KNOW YOURSELF

Everyone has natural strengths and weaknesses. There is power in knowing what yours are. When you know what your value is, you can make skilled contributions to your team. You can put yourself in positions, consciously, where you'll thrive. Likewise, when you know what your less-than-stellar tendencies are, you can be prepared to mitigate them.

If you have the inclination, take a personality test or two, and think through your own strengths and specific blind spots. Ask others to support you in understanding how you operate in interactions with others. Be mindful that you'll need to know your style, and also to step out of your style sometimes to act in ways that may be more challenging. Flexing your personality takes more energy and will feel less natural, but we all have to do it sometimes. You may not like your laundry room or want to do laundry today, but if you have no more clean clothes, you've got to get in there and do the work.

Your brain works differently than your coworker's, and that's beautiful. Difference is a positive, and it's important not to stereotype any one natural style. They're all important.

If you can better understand how you work as an individual, you'll have a better idea of how to get out from under your impulsive limbic system, and into considered thought.

ORGANIZATIONAL CULTURE MATTERS TOO

When making a judgment call, take into consideration not only your own tendencies and preferences but also that of the organization. You can make the best decision in the world, but if the culture of your organization doesn't support it, it will still fail.

As the old quote from Peter Drucker says, "Culture eats strategy for breakfast." Ensure your culture can support the decision.

WHAT'S NEXT?

Of course, most decisions aren't made by only one person. As we've learned, collaboration is key even in a small-scale personal decision. Inviting people to the table who think differently than you is critical, in any decision. At work, though, there are inevitably many stakeholders involved, and complex decision roles to navigate. How you approach decision-making there, will depend not only on your personality and decision style but also your role. Are you the driver of the decision, or the decision-maker? Are you providing input?

In the next chapter, we'll discuss what these decision

roles are, and why they matter. It takes a team to make a good decision.

CHAPTER THREE

DECISION-MAKING ROLES

ONE OF THE ROOT CAUSES OF THE AIR FORCE'S FAILED
ECSS project was the Department of Defense decision-making. There were many decision-makers and stakeholders with
varied interests and expectations. However, the decision-making roles could have been much better defined.

There are many reasons for such a grand-scale program
failure, but we would argue that poor decision-making structure was key. Solid decisions made more quickly may have set
the project up for success. Decision-making was important
throughout project execution, but the most important decision,
the one to cancel the project, should have been made much
sooner.

The project did not have clear governance or executive
sponsorship within the Air Force. Who was doing what, when
it was being done, and budget management was being delegated
as best they could. However, without an executive sponsor, they
were missing a key piece of oversight. In a well-run project,
the executive sponsor has more authority than the program
or project manager. They are able to intervene when an issue

occurs, or when parts of the program go outside of budget or scope. Unfortunately, for the majority of the eight years of the program, there was no clear executive sponsor to escalate to. When a problem occurred beyond the program manager's ability to solve, or when a decision needed to be made beyond their authority to make it, they had no recourse.

This was a huge undertaking, and decision-making authority was unevenly distributed and poorly outlined. There were multiple potential decision-makers and stakeholders for multiple aspects of the system. Unclear expectations and competing interests made the outcomes overwhelming and confusing. During most of the project, it was not clear who the final decision-maker was for different decisions. Worse, the limited decision-makers who did exist rotated so frequently that it added to the confusion. People often left were promoted, stepped down, or moved on, vacating their spot and taking important program knowledge with them.

When a high-impact decision is being made, it's critical to define roles. This is also important when implementing programs or projects, as implementation will inevitably mean more impactful decisions along the way. The Institute for Defense Analyses performed an independent study on the project and issued a report.[18] Among other concerns, they cited a lack of basic requirements for successful implementation. One of the key elements they were missing? "Having a single accountable leader who has the authority and willingness to exercise the authority to enforce all necessary changes to the

---

18   Benjamin S. Aronin et al., *Expeditionary Combat Support System: Root Cause Analysis* (Alexandria, VA: Institute for Defense Analyses, October 2011), https://www.acq.osd.mil/asda/ae/ada/docs/2011-ida-rca-ecss-p-4732.pdf.

business required for successful fielding of the software."[19] As risks were identified, or issues developed, no one had the authority to resolve them. No one had the authority to decrease the scope.

To be fair, the project could have been doomed from the beginning. The performance expectations of the system were unrealistic to the extreme. The project was estimated to be twenty-eight times larger than any ERP system previously in existence, and rather than pilot it, or commit to an Agile implementation with small slices—they went all in with that billion dollars.

All in all, a billion dollars in taxpayer money was wasted, partly because of this major breakdown in decision-making roles.

A HELPFUL FRAMEWORK

When you know an important decision is coming up the pike, everyone involved should sit down and ensure they're speaking the same language. The group should identify who will be stepping into the key decision-making roles, and all agree to those roles. Clarity is project (and job) saving.

For the sake of clarity, we'd like to introduce you to a helpful framework: DIDI. The DIDI acronym as described below provides an important starting point for a conversation about roles. It is not exhaustive. You may need to tweak the framework to add additional roles, or to rename it using the language of your organization. The point is not the exact structure, but rather the conversation to be had within it. Assuming that certain

---

19   Gary R. Bliss, "Root Cause Analysis of the Expeditionary Combat Support System Program," US Department of Defense, August 28, 2013.

people will take on certain tasks without talking about them is how you go down a slippery slope of wasting time and money.

DEFINING ROLES

Now let's discuss how these roles might break out in high-impact decisions. Each role accomplishes important and defined functions in the decision-making process, and there are responsibilities associated with each.

In the case of a single individual making a personal decision, he or she may be able to fill all of the roles themselves. (Though it's still wise to seek out additional input, as discussed earlier in the book, to fill in your blind spots.) It's also possible for one person to fill two or three roles but not the others. The larger and more complex the decision is, and the more people it affects, the larger the odds of all of these roles being filled by different people.

Decision-Making Roles: DIDI

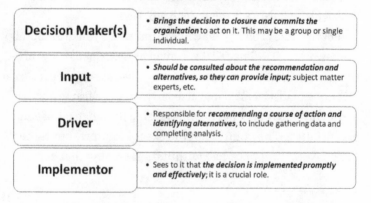

Decision Maker(s)	• *Brings the decision to closure and commits the organization* to act on it. This may be a group or single individual.
Input	• *Should be consulted about the recommendation and alternatives, so they can provide input;* subject matter experts, etc.
Driver	• Responsible for *recommending a course of action and identifying alternatives*, to include gathering data and completing analysis.
Implementor	• Sees to it that *the decision is implemented promptly and effectively*; it is a crucial role.

D IS FOR DECISION-MAKER

The decision-maker is the person or people who bring the decision to closure and commit themselves and/or the organization to acting on it. In some cases, a team of people makes a decision jointly, like a Board of Directors or a group of subject matter experts. In other cases, it's a single individual. (We do not recommend a two-person decision team, but three, or five people will work. See Chapter Nine.)

The decision-maker's authority should be aligned with the decision being made. In other words, it's possible for a junior person to make an organizational decision if that decision impacts their specific job or department. If they have the authority, and the ability to commit to action, they can make even a high-impact decision on the right level. The key idea is authority, which changes depending on the organization.

For example, Amazon customer service people seem to have little authority, as Kandis once went through two escalations to get a $15 credit for a mistake made by the company, which negatively impacted her (the customer). In contrast, the Zappos customer service team members are famously granted the authority to solve the customer's problem, hence their first core value, "Deliver WOW Through Service." They are empowered to make decisions and commit to follow-up actions due to the clarity of their role.

Regardless of the level of the decision-maker, they need to be committed to making timely decisions. Otherwise, they will run into analysis paralysis, lose opportunities, or both. In the pandemic, organizations that were able to make swift decisions to pivot strategically survived. The ones who made the wrong decision, or spent months and years not making decisions, did not. Many of them don't have their lights on and doors open anymore.

As the proverb says, "When opportunity knocks, it doesn't knock twice."

I IS FOR INPUT

The input role provides valuable contributions on which way the decision should go. Every organization will have important stakeholders, who will have information or influence that will need to be taken into account. Who should be consulted for input may change depending on the type of decision and the leading options on the table.

Input should always include subject matter experts. If there's a decision that includes people, HR should weigh in. For a computer platform implementation, the Information Technology team should be consulted. If that platform is intended to support customer service, you will want to include at least one customer service representative.

To determine who should provide input, sit down and think through the decision in depth. Consider people who have: influence, interest, and/or are impacted by a decision.

Who Are the People Interested in the Decision?

It can be **important to determine if stakeholders are supportive, resistant, unaware, or neutral when it comes to their interest in a decision.** This group may not be directly impacted by the decision, however, there may be dependencies or potential downstream implications that capture their interest.

Who Are the People That Can Influence the Decision?

These are the people who don't directly make the decision, but can certainly keep it from succeeding or guide it in a specific direction. Generally, there is some level of authority or power associated with stakeholders who can influence a decision. Including HR or your legal department's perspective early is wise risk mitigation.

It can also be an important strategy to double-check. If the CEO believes your decision won't square with the organization's direction, she will shut it down in implementation if not before.

Who Is Impacted by the Decision?

To return to the customer service platform example, you really do need to consult with customer service during the decision-making stage. Their input is the difference between success and failure. The on-the-ground understanding of the daily realities of the job should drive the requirements of the system to ensure success. Perhaps even more importantly, you will need customer service professionals to "buy in" to the solution. Consulting key players early will dramatically improve their participation in implementation.

Failing to include all stakeholders can cause unintended consequences. Influencers can identify risks and opportunities that the decision-makers and decision drivers have not considered. Without them, bad outcomes are far more likely.

Work closely with these people as you brainstorm possible solutions, and then make the decision.

THE SECOND D IS FOR DRIVER OF THE DECISION

In large organizations, executives function as decision-making machines. Despite this function, they do not have time to spend ten to thirty hours getting all of the information and consulting all of the roles providing inputs. That's where the driver comes in.

The driver of the decision is responsible for moving the decision process forward. There must be one person ultimately held accountable, though they may work with a team.

The driver does the legwork. As a result, they will develop not only a primary recommendation but also alternatives to present to the decision-maker. It is their responsibility to do the work to get the decision-maker to the best possible solution.

Say your boss comes to you with an assignment. "We've got a problem. Sales are way down. I need you to go out and figure out the problem, and come back to me by next Friday. Present three courses of action on how we get our sales up, and tell me which one you recommend. I'm going to want solid data on all three options." In this example, the driver of the decision is *you*.

Since the decision driver is responsible for the process, you will need to consult others, brainstorm, gather information, and analyze that information. The driver is responsible for putting together the packaged recommendations for the decision at the end.

Without the decision-maker role, the driver goes nowhere, but a decision-maker without a driver is grasping in the dark.

I IS FOR IMPLEMENTER

This role is particularly crucial for high-impact decisions. This person ensures that the decision is implemented properly and effectively.

In the context of an organization, most high-impact decisions result in implementation via a formal project. When that happens, the implementer may also be called a project manager. They will manage the time, scope, cost, resources, quality, and change management resulting from the decision. Their role is to focus on questions like, "Who's doing what and when?" "How will this be communicated?" "How is risk going to be identified and managed throughout?"

Implementation in large projects will normally require many people to be involved. It's still critical that there be one person ultimately responsible for successful outcomes. (If everyone is responsible, no one is responsible. Have you ever tried to plan a family Thanksgiving without a keeper of the menu? You'd end up with a dozen pots of mashed potatoes.)

Selecting the one person in charge of implementation will, in large part, be driven by the solution. If the decision is focused on technology, perhaps the implementer is the IT director. Or, given their newfound expertise, it may be the driver of the decision. You should always select the best person to shepherd the project from start to finish.

It is critical to choose an implementer. The making of a decision exists at a single point on a timeline. If no one is put in charge of implementation, mass chaos and confusion will begin immediately. Without follow-through, you're sunk before you start swimming. A decision without action is no decision at all.

While this may seem obvious, we cannot tell you the number of times we have been in meetings where this has been an issue. A decision is made in the meeting. Then, everyone leaves the room and...no action. Two weeks later, someone asks about the decision that was made and what's next. Everyone shrugs their shoulders, and it all stays the same. Appointing an implementer in that meeting ensures that someone is immediately driving the project forward.

Bring your implementer into the process early so they can know exactly when to lace up, and hit the ground running.

THE IMPORTANCE OF ROLES

Unclear roles and responsibilities can slow down decisions and prevent problems from being addressed. They can cost you employee engagement. Unclear roles and responsibilities tend to lead to major problems in projects and frustration. People leave. Even if you solve the problem, those people may be gone forever.

Know your role in high-impact decisions. Even more importantly, be sure to communicate clear roles and responsibilities to every person involved in the decision. It is the one step that will make or break the decision as a whole.

WHY CLARITY MATTERS

Knowing who has what decision-making role is profoundly important, regardless of the type of decision.

The clarity in roles expedites decisions. It also protects morale. People who are providing input will not think they are making the decision, and get angry when it turns out they're not. The decision driver will grasp the responsibility and push the decision process forward.

Clarity prevents overstepping. It also removes complacency, where people don't realize they have the authority to make a needed decision. It creates a clear sense of ownership and responsibility for the decisions that must be made. When more than one decision-maker is in play, they will be aware of each other and will know to collaborate or to decide in parallel, appropriately.

The roles must be clearly defined, and the roles in relation to the authority must be defined. Someone might act one way in terms of a one-off decision, and another in terms of ongoing responsibility and a specific process. In fact, it's common to have ongoing responsibility up to a certain level of authority, and then have to escalate and drive a one-off decision with your boss. If there's a routine process, you can successfully operate with all of the hats.

COMPLEX DECISIONS CAN MEAN MANY ROLES

Decision-Making Roles: DIDI

Decision Maker(s)	• *Kandis*
Input	• *Poison Control, Veterinarian Tech, Veterinarian, Kandis' husband*
Driver	• *Kandis*
Implementor	• *Veterinarian, Veterinarian Tech*

Kandis has a dog, whom she loves. His name is Coffee Dog. (That's a story for another time.) For any of you non-pet owners out there, a person's love for their animal rivals a parent's love for their child. It's big. So when Kandis came home one day after work to find Coffee Dog acting sickly, and an empty packet of Starbucks chocolate-covered espresso beans abandoned nearby, she freaked out.

Guilt and panic hit her hard. Why did she leave the bag of beans unattended in her open backpack? Why hadn't she thought ahead?

She could have gotten stuck here. If Kandis didn't have a long track record of navigating high-pressure situations and making cool decisions in the midst of them, she might have.

WHEN YOU'RE THE 2 D'S (DRIVER AND DECISION-MAKER)

Kandis knew she couldn't navigate the situation from a place of emotion. She would have to be the decision driver and the decision-maker. However, there were many other important roles that needed to be included in the decision-making process, especially the subject matter experts that needed to weigh in on how to best treat Coffee Dog and those who would implement the solution.

Her intent was to get Coffee Dog healthy again (*decision intent* is key, no matter the decision) but she lacked information. As an experienced decision-maker (and dedicated dog mom) she knew that what she needed next was input.

Getting Input

She started by calling the animal poison control hotline. They asked her to weigh Coffee Dog and read the Starbucks packaging, in order to figure out if the amount he had eaten was dangerous for his size. The numbers didn't look good. She was told to take him to the emergency vet immediately.

That was her first line of input. She got enough information from an expert to know: this is an emergency.

She packed up Coffee Dog while she called the vet tech at the emergency vet. Input source number two. The tech agreed with poison control. "You need to drop him off curbside *now*."

Kandis did as she was told. She dropped Coffee Dog at the

emergency vet. All of the input had pointed in the same direction, and now all she had to do was wait.

It was less than an hour later when Kandis got the phone call from the emergency veterinarian on duty. All hope was not lost. There was a course of action. This would be input source number three. He gave his recommendation. The price tag was hard to stomach. It would be thousands of dollars just to start treatment. Did she want to spend that money over a five-dollar bag of chocolate espresso beans? No. She was angry with herself and upset. The decision was now in front of her.

She couldn't leave Coffee Dog in distress.

Weighing Options

Kandis made a smart move when faced with a high-impact decision: she asked if there were other options. The veterinarian said there were a few. (There almost always are.) Each had risks, benefits, and costs. Bottom line: all options included getting the expresso beans out of Coffee Dog's system at the soonest, to get his heart rate down. The follow-up care is where the options came in.

Her options were as follows, listed in order of the most expensive to the least expensive option.

Option 1: Initiate vomiting, insert an IV to keep him hydrated and administer medications, and keep Coffee Dog for observation for seventy-two hours, monitoring his vitals around the clock.

Option 2: Initiate vomiting and keep Coffee Dog for twenty-four hours, monitoring his vitals around the clock, ensuring he was eating normally and stable before he was released.

Option 3: Initiate vomiting, get Coffee Dog's heart rate down to a normal range, and send him home for monitoring (he was not to be left alone) for a minimum of twenty-four hours after release. Provide instructions for easing him back onto solid foods.

After she hung up, Kandis stared at her steering wheel. It was 2:10 a.m. on a Saturday. The vet informed her that she had fifteen minutes to make a decision, so they could continue to treat Coffee Dog. Decision-makers are often faced with compressed timelines, but this was extreme. She called her husband, who was out of town, for one last source of input. They talked it through, weighing their options, considering risks, benefits, and their ideal outcome. By the time they hung up, Kandis was ready to make her final decision.

The Final I (Implementer)

Kandis called the veterinarian with her decision. The vet would be the implementer of the decision moving forward. As we'll cover in later chapters, this moment after the decision is made can feel like the end of the road, but really it's just the beginning. Once a course of action has been decided on, then the real work begins. In a medical crisis, the stakes of implementation are clear: the success of the decision relies entirely on the success of implementation. Either the strategy would work, and Coffee Dog would recover or...the unthinkable.

They agreed on when he would next communicate the status of Coffee Dog, and what to do if he needed to change the course of action at any point during the night.

Ongoing Decision Making

They all made it through the night—Coffee Dog, Kandis, her husband, and the vet. Things seemed to be moving in the right direction. Kandis was even allowed to bring Coffee Dog home the next day. They were in the clear. Or so they thought.

When Coffee Dog came home he seemed much better. However, later that same night Kandis realized he was starting to suffer from partial paralyzation. It's not uncommon, in the implementation phase for hiccups to occur. Unseen challenges. For Kandis and Coffee Dog, there were even more decisions to make.

She took Coffee Dog back to the vet to do more blood work. His enzymes were still elevated and had had inflammation. The vet prescribed medication to bring down his enzyme levels and reduce the inflammation, which worked at first, but soon after the initial prescription, Coffee Dog started throwing up. Kandis had to take him back to the vet twice more for different courses of action.

What began as a single decision—choosing the best course of action to get Coffee Dog out of this crisis—became a series of decisions over several weeks. Each decision shared the same single intent of getting Coffee Dog healthy again. At all points Kandis had to work within all of these roles: she had to Drive, gather Input, make a Decision, and appoint an Implementer. Not every high-impact decision is a one-off. Many high-impact situations, like Coffee Dog's crisis, will require ongoing decisions. Being clear on which role(s) you are filling will become critical as you adjust to rapidly changing situations in real-time.

DECISION POINTS

Decision making is not always a linear process with the luxury of time. Sometimes, like the situation with Kandis's dog, decisions will need to be made quickly and in sequence. In these cases, it's important to have a clear sense of your intent or your

Commander's Intent. (Don't worry, we'll get to the Commander's Intent in decision-making later.) Choosing your course of action will become easier under pressure if your goal is clear.

The Army describes a "decision point" as the moment you anticipate making a key decision concerning a specific course of action. You may face many decision points to get to your ideal end state. This is also true of organizational projects, particularly in implementation. Going through a quick version of the entire decision-making process can be extremely helpful, as is keeping clear roles.

Clear decision roles lead to faster, more efficient decision-making. Without them, no decision can be made. The course of action can never change, or decisions will get made at the inappropriate authority level, without enough information. People who make those decisions will fight with each other. The left hand will not talk to the right hand, and failure becomes increasingly likely.

DELEGATING AUTHORITY FOR DECISION MAKING

There are several ways to empower people with decision-making authority, depending on the organization's choices. Here are a few common examples.

One of the organizations Kandis works with has delegated authority to the Executive Director to make decisions up to $50,000. More than that and the Board of Directors will need to approve the expense. For example, if the Executive Director wants to purchase a new company vehicle, they will likely have to present all the facts associated with it, prove they've done their due diligence, and the Board of Directors will sign off. The Executive Director also tends to delegate their authority to directors under them. Department heads can approve decisions up to a cost of $15,000, and supervisors under them can approve up to $1,500. It cascades down from there.

Well-delegated authority empowers people to make decisions at the appropriate level and prevents bottlenecks. If an Executive Director had to sign off anytime anyone below him/her in the organization spent a single cent, very few purchases would be made. Work would grind to a halt. Entrusting people with authority is critical to realistic organizational function.

Authority can be given based on dollar amounts, but it can also be given in other ways. One person can be given "go or no go" decision-making power on projects. It can also be based on the level of effort. If a project requires up to ten full-time people for six months, someone can greenlight it. Eleven people for seven months need a higher level of approval. Some companies don't have budgets assigned to any of their projects. They forecast work and timelines based on full-time employee headcount alone.

Authority can be delegated not just based on how many resources, but also on the timing or type of decision.

AUTHORITY FOR TYPES OF DECISIONS

A given person can be empowered to make decisions in one of three situations. First, someone can be charged with one-off, specific decisions. Alternatively, they can have authority for ongoing responsibilities, or routine processes.

One-Off Decisions

One-off decisions fall under one intent. They may require one decision, such as the decision to buy a specific car or to move to a new city. Or, they can require a series of decisions, such as Kandis's situation with Coffee Dog. Increasing sales numbers could be another example of a "one-off." If sales numbers have dipped below an identified threshold, increasing them will presumably resolve the situation and allow you to return your attention to other variables.

Position-Specific Responsibilities

Position-specific responsibilities are just what they sound like. When, in our previous example, the Board of Directors empowered the Executive Director to make decisions up to $50,000, the director had ongoing authority as part of her job. She will always be able to make decisions up to that level. If the director moves on to another organization, the new director will be charged with this same responsibility. The authority stays in the position. Hiring authority is another example of a position-specific responsibility.

Other roles may also be inherent to a position. A project manager may not be able to make a large out-of-the-ordinary funding decision. However, they will most likely be expected to be the driver of that decision. If another project manager is hired, it will be important that their authority and role expectations be communicated clearly. If not, you're setting them up for difficulty and lack of clarity.

Position-specific responsibility is a strong way to set up authority. It drives consistency and removes confusion. When people need to expedite a decision, they know exactly who to go to. They have worked with this same person before on this exact type of decision, so they know what type of information to assemble.

Routine Processes

A routine process is an ongoing series of steps with inputs and a specific output. Processes normally have built-in decision points. Routine processes will need to have clear decision roles defined for each decision point. (This is normally done by someone with higher-level authority in the organization.)

For example, the medical device industry has to go through clinical trials before a given device can be approved. Every time a new clinical trial is set up, there is a process to run that trial. Decisions are needed in several steps.

The device manufacturer will need to decide which participants can participate in each phase of the clinical trial. What specific criteria should be used? They may consider age range, male versus female, and other qualifiers, such as being a heart patient for a cardiac device. They will also need to decide which medical facilities to invite to participate and in what region. Where are they likely to find enough participants who meet the protocol? The company will also want to consider specific ethical and operational factors. Every time they develop a new device and get a trial approved, they will have to repeat the process. The decisions themselves will change, but the decision points remain the same.

At each decision point, a different person may be responsible for that decision. Perhaps Sally is charged with selecting the research sites for all clinical trials within a small organization, as she has the most insight into the geographical locations and the local populations, in addition to the facilities and equipment. Sally isn't charged with making the site-selection decisions based on her role, per se, but because of the knowledge and experience, she possesses.

When it comes to routine process roles, we recommend the organization create a visual process map. (You may wish to research how Six Sigma practitioners create process maps, for reference.) If making a decision is an important step in the process, it needs to be represented on the visual. Which person or position will be making that particular decision should also be clearly communicated. If the person changes depending on circumstances, it's crucial to define circumstances.

The goal of process mapping is for a layperson, uninitiated in the specifics of your task, to understand what's supposed to happen and when. The fastest way to break a process is to fail to make decision points clear. Map them out and save yourself from the unnecessary heartache of communication failure.

WHAT'S NEXT?

Up to this point, we have discussed general decision-making strategies. In Part Two, we will go through the step-by-step process we recommend for high-impact decisions. This process will be much less effective without the strategies in Part One. The two parts build on each other.

This intensive process is not appropriate for every decision. It would be a waste of time to go through the entire process for a trivial decision like what you will have for lunch. That decision has almost no impact on tomorrow. This process is for high-impact decisions.

How, then, should we define a "high-impact" decision that will need the full process? The term means different things to different people. It will look different across organizations, based on their missions and risk tolerance. For one organization, $10,000 is impactful, and for another, $10 million. The key is that high-impact decisions cannot easily be reversed. They have a significant effect on the person or organization. They are worth hours of consideration.

Some decisions are trivial and some of them are life-changing. Know the difference. Use an abbreviated version of the full process if that suits your purposes. Use the steps at your discretion. Do the legwork that makes sense for your situation. Now, let's begin. Turn the page, and learn how to make high-impact decisions.

PART TWO

THE DECISION PROCESS, STEP BY STEP

(1)	Define decision & successful outcomes	(2)	Gather information
(3)	Identify options	(4)	Prioritize options
(5)	Gain buy-in	(6)	Make decision
(7)	Implement decision	(8)	Review decision

CHAPTER FOUR

STEP ONE

DEFINE DECISION & SUCCESSFUL OUTCOMES

A FEW YEARS AGO, LEARNIT NEEDED TO IMPLEMENT A new performance management system. Damon spent a lot of time coming up with clear expectations around what the system would need to accomplish.

The big-picture goal was to create a transparent and consistent structure. It would help set compensation guidelines on merit-based raises. It would house performance evaluations, and help to determine promotions. Ideally, the system would support either coaching up or coaching out lower-performing team members.

He also wanted systems and processes to help managers invest in their employees via consistent one-on-one meetings, track goals, and allow for timeline planning. Having a place where praise could be highlighted for employees would be helpful. The system should also ideally help measure overall employee engagement. The total project needed to come in under a specified budget.

Damon appointed someone to fulfill these marching orders. They would have a large amount of freedom and flexibility in achieving these goals. They could pick software, the cadence of meetings, and create any structure they wanted, so long as they fully accomplished what was needed.

PAINTING A PICTURE OF SUCCESS

The first step to any successful decision is defining what success looks like. If you understand the intent of the decision and define a good outcome, the mechanics of making the right decision become much easier.

There are thousands of performance management systems out there. How could anyone vet them without having a sense of what is needed?

Without clear criteria for success, and understanding of why the decision is being made, anyone driving the decision will fail. If you don't give good guidance on success, your team may spend large amounts of time going through a decision process and come back with an option that's not in line with your goals. That's on you.

Putting in the work upfront sets your team (and you) up for success.

What exactly does the definition of success look like? There are two components: the success criteria, and the Commander's Intent. Let's start with a simple exercise to get you thinking about success criteria.

THE FUTURE PRESS RELEASE

This is an exercise created by some folks at Amazon. It's brilliant.

Whenever you are beginning a new project, opening up a new location, or facing a new decision, try this exercise. Sit down with the entire team responsible. Together, you'll brainstorm and write a press release as if it were one to three years in the future and you're looking back on your accomplishments.

The press release will inevitably talk about the goals that were set and accomplished and the success that came as a result. Many people even like to reference challenges that came along the way and how they overcame them.

Guidelines for writing your future press release:

1. Start with a clear headline: Your headline should be attention grabbing and highlight the main message of your press release.
2. Provide context: Provide some background information on the topic you're writing about. Explain why it's important and relevant.
3. Make predictions: Use your knowledge of the subject matter to make predictions. Be specific and provide evidence to support your claims. Include statistics and data to back up your claims and make your predictions more concrete.
4. Use quotes: Including quotes from experts or relevant stakeholders can add credibility to your predictions. Make sure to give proper attribution to the quotes.
5. Keep it concise: Try to work within 500 words. Make every word count by "boiling it down" to the most important information.

The exercise gets people thinking about the future through a completely different lens. It makes it easier to define a logical plan for how to accomplish goals. By having it on paper, it becomes easier to benchmark success in the future.

FOCUSING EFFORT

Use the future press release as a tool to focus your decisions and efforts. For example, recently the Learnit team decided internally that they wanted to start a branded podcast interviewing instructors and clients. It sounded great. Reality has constraints, though. Learnit is a small company, and they don't have unlimited resources. Any resources put into the podcast would be taken away from other projects.

Damon had the team go through the exercise of the future press release. They came back two weeks later with a two-page release. It described a realistic picture of success, including half a million subscribers. From there, Damon and the team could walk back to what resources would be required to build to that point, which would require at least one piece of new content per week. Would this investment meet their other goals? Would it be a better choice than alternatives? (In this case, no.)

Seven out of ten times when Learnit does a future press release, it doesn't move forward. The team is unable to articulate the goals, or the goals don't fit into the vision of where the company is going at that moment. The exercise focuses the team on what success looks like, and that creates a method of talking about big decisions in a new way. Even if the project moves on to other steps in the decision-making process (see the next chapters), having gone through the clear definition of success is powerful.

SOLVING THE RIGHT PROBLEM

Once you've thought through your success criteria, it's time to start thinking critically about the problem at hand. Have you found the real problem or opportunity? Or is there a different or deeper issue to deal with? This thinking cannot be rushed.

If we're talking about the performance management system, what's the real issue? Do you need the system because supervisors and employees are not having one-on-one meetings? Or is the issue that employees are disengaged? Does the team need a platform to assist with tracking their personal development and goals? The difference matters. You don't want to end up with a system that documents feedback and meetings well but continues to have disengaged employees.

For every solution, there is a root problem. (See the excellent book *Upstream* by Dan Heath.) If the issue is that employees are disengaged, why is that? Maybe the company lacks a story or vision that people connect with. Maybe it's the lack of clear expectations. Maybe people aren't talking to each other sufficiently.

You don't want to make a significant investment in time and money, only to find out you've made your issue worse or solved the wrong problem.

CREATING A PROBLEM STATEMENT

To create a problem statement, you need three simple elements:

1. DEFINE THE CURRENT STATE

Think through your problem. Can you describe it in enough detail that someone unfamiliar with the issue could understand what you're experiencing?

Paint a clear picture of the problem state. Write it down. Be specific.

2. DESCRIBE THE SUCCESSFUL END STATE

If this problem were to be resolved to your exact specifications, what would that look like? Again, be detailed. Use the Future Press Release exercise to get your creative juices flowing if you're having trouble visualizing success. Write it clearly, and paint the full picture.

3. DEFINE THE GAP

Take a look at your current state and your successful end state. Where is the gap between these two realities? How is that gap affecting you, your business, and your team? Does it feel insurmountable? Is it a chasm that requires an enormous bridge, or do you feel capable of hopping the gap in a few simple steps? The more specific you can be about where you are versus where you're going, the easier it will be to take action later on.

Let's return to our performance management system for a real-world example.

4. DEFINE THE CURRENT STATE

Routine performance conversations are not happening between employees and managers. Employees aren't being recognized for desired behaviors or penalized for poor performance. Zero documentation exists for either, which means no accountability. High levels of attrition.

5. DESCRIBE THE SUCCESSFUL END STATE

A one-stop-shop for performance management, with well-thought-out goals down to the individual contributor level. Managers are meeting with each of their direct reports biweekly, documenting the discussion and outlining clear action items. Timely performance feedback is being given and often. There has been a change in the culture, from the leaders on down. Employees are being trained on new systems. There is an increased level of trust and motivation across the organization, increasing retention by 5 percent. Surveys are consistently showing employee engagement at 87+ percent.

6. DEFINE THE GAP

Employees operating beyond expectations aren't growing, and some underperformers are skating by. Top performers aren't being appropriately recognized or compensated, and they may leave. Managers haven't been trained on conducting successful one-on-one meetings nor do they have a platform to document the meetings in. Employee engagement surveys are not being conducted at routine intervals throughout the year.

When you have a clearly delineated problem statement, your next step will be identifying and writing the Commander's Intent.

COMMUNICATING COMMANDER'S INTENT

The Commander's Intent is a concept from the military. It's defined as:[20]

---

20 Department of the Army, *ADP 5-0: The Operations Process* (Washington, DC: Department of the Army, July 2019), 9, https://armypubs.army.mil/epubs/DR_pubs/DR_a/ARN18126-ADP_5-0-000-WEB-3.pdf.

The commander's intent is a clear and concise expression of the purpose of the operation and the desired military end state that supports mission command, provides focus to the staff, and helps subordinate and supporting commanders act to achieve the commander's desired results without further orders, even when the operation does not unfold as planned.

The intent isn't optional. The driver and the rest of the team need to understand *why* a decision is being made and what it is intended to accomplish. So will you. That way, when the metaphorical bombs start dropping, everyone can make good decisions to adjust to changing circumstances. Otherwise, the team will blindly follow orders or wait for clarification. Or, they may choose to pivot in an unhelpful direction. Try to ensure your intent is SMART: Specific, Measurable, Attainable, Relevant, and Timebound.

When creating a problem statement, you don't want to just do a great job of describing the successful end state (Step Two) on paper, you must successfully communicate it to others. This allows the team to stay laser focused on outcomes and course correct along the way.

As Mike Tyson says, "Everybody has a strategy until you get punched in the face." Commander's Intent empowers people to continue working toward the desired end state, even when the path to get there changes.

PERSONAL EXAMPLES

Let's revisit Coffee Dog's trip to the vet. Here is what the same exercise might look like in that case:

Step 1. Current State: Coffee Dog's liver enzymes are still extremely high. If his blood work is not within normal ranges, it could be disease or possible organ damage, which could ultimately shorten his lifespan, perhaps drastically. (Kandis does not want Coffee Dog's life shortened, ever.)

Step 2. Successful End State: A healthy dog with all of his blood work within normal ranges.

Step 3. Gap: Medical care and treatment plan to evaluate his diet, treats, and supplements, and continue to test and treat until his blood work is back in normal ranges.

The Commander's Intent as a result might look like this:

Continue holistic treatment at the vet and with diet changes until Coffee Dog's blood work is back within normal ranges, ASAP and certainly within three months. (Kandis explicitly refused to add a budget to the statement, which is also an expression of intent!)

At the beginning of every decision-making meeting, it's worthwhile to have a slide with your Commander's Intent written on it.

The Commander's Intent contains the key information you or your team will need to make new decisions if and when the situation changes. The more you can describe your desired outcomes after the problem is solved, the better and more useful your intent will be.

Of course, to write a good problem statement and a good statement of the Commander's Intent, it is important to know that you're solving the right problem and not just the symptoms. What is the root cause, and how exactly do you find it?

FINDING THE ROOT CAUSE

Many times, the person who gets praised in the organization is the one who is constantly putting out fires. Those aren't the ones you should be praising. They are treating symptoms.

Instead, the person to praise is the one who identifies what is causing the fires in the first place. If you figure out the real issue driving the problem or leading to the decision, you will eliminate most of the need for firefighting in the first place.

A root cause is a factor that causes a particular situation or the fundamental reason for a problem occurring. Does searching out the root cause take a little effort? Sure. Is it worth it? Absolutely. The time and effort you'll save in the long run by making sure you truly understand the situation in-depth is worth its weight.

There are many tools you can use to help you analyze a situation to find a root cause. We will highlight two of them: the fishbone diagram, and the affinity diagram.

THE FISHBONE DIAGRAM

The fishbone diagram focuses on cause and effect and gets its name from its shape. The problem sits in the head of the fish. Then, you consider all of the possible factors that cause or contribute to the problem. Those are written into the "bones." The tool is also famous as the Ishikawa diagram by the name of its creator Kaoru Ishikawa. Here's an example.

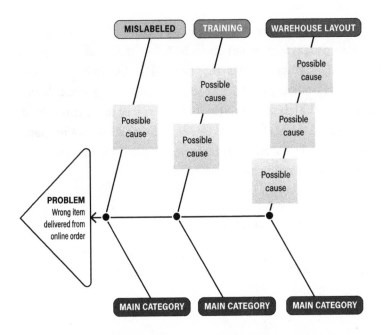

To fill in the fishbone diagram, you will need to brainstorm. "What might be causing this?" "How could that be happening?" "Why?"

For example, Damon recently ordered a mattress online. Instead of the mattress, they delivered a bed frame. Those are two completely different products. He was confused, to say the least.

Say you're the mattress company, and you receive this complaint from the customer, with pictures. It's your job to figure out what happened so it does not happen again. How could they have been sent the wrong product? Maybe the box was mislabeled. Or, maybe the barcode was tagged incorrectly in the scanning software. Perhaps training is an issue. Are there other human factors? Maybe someone didn't follow the correct process and shipped the wrong product. Is the warehouse layout confusing?

Once you have some ideas, you can drill down further, adding ideas further out on each "bone." If each of the ideas is the effect, what would be the cause? If the box was mislabeled, were the labels printed correctly and put on the wrong boxes, or were the labels printed incorrectly? Does the scanning software have a bug or process issue? Was a new hire not properly onboarded? Through brainstorming, you continue until you feel you've established the root cause.

THE AFFINITY DIAGRAM

To lead a group brainstorm using an affinity diagram approach, first, write the problem that you're trying to solve on a whiteboard or on a slide.[21]

---

21 The term "Affinity Diagram" was devised by Jiro Kawakita in the 1960s and is sometimes referred to as the KJ Method.

Affinity Diagram

Problem: Project Milestones Consistently Late

GROUP 1: TRAINING	GROUP 2: LEADERSHIP	GROUP 3: PROCESSES	GROUP 4: TECHNOLOGY	GROUP 5: CULTURE
Not trained to process	Confusion with leadership roles	Process outdated for ABC	Not everyone has license to software	No sense of urgency
Onboarding too short	Too many people providing guidance	No process exists for XYZ	No standardized way to use software	People are not held accountable
Don't know how to use project management software	Project Manager has no authority over team	Process is confusing	Project management software doesn't integrate with other systems	Team members consistently overworked

For this example, you are trying to figure out why projects are running late. You will ask the group members to brainstorm individually.

Perhaps people don't have sufficient training in project management. Maybe leadership is not sponsoring the project appropriately. Maybe you don't have good processes, tools, or the right technology. Maybe the culture of the organization is to "wing it."

Each person will write ideas, one by one, on sticky notes. Then, they'll post those notes on the board, whether a physical board for in-person meetings or a tool like Miro for remote meetings. The sticky notes will sit in an unordered tangle on the board.

Then, you will group the notes according to likeness. Maybe three or four of the sticky notes point to training issues. Another five might address the process. After the notes are grouped, each group should be labeled. Then, everyone at the meeting will discuss each group of ideas. Your goal is for the discussion to lead to an accurate identification of the root cause or causes.

If possible, have individuals come up with their ideas on their sticky notes before posting them in the group. There will inevitably be new ideas that arise in the discussion, and that's fine. Having a little less guidance as to the category in the beginning, though, tends to lead to more divergent creative thinking. You don't want to start with groupthink.[22]

COMBINING TOOLS

It is possible to combine tools as needed. You can brainstorm affinities with the group and then jointly use those affinities to fill out a fishbone diagram. Use the tools that are the best fit for your situation.

KNOWING WHEN YOU'RE DONE

Keep asking why and using diagrams until you feel like you have an answer. Collaborate with others as needed. After a brainstorming session, you may need to do investigative work to confirm assumptions. Your chosen root cause will drive how

---

22 A practice that manufactures consensus by coming to a decision as a group in a way that discourages creativity and individual responsibility (intentionally or unintentionally).

gather information. (See Chapter Five.) However, if it turns ᵗ that the data does not support your assumed root cause, you'll come back to this step. Repeat the process as many times as necessary until you understand the real problem.

It's always worth the time and effort to identify the real root cause. If you're not solving the right problem, you may be able to slap some bandages on here and there, but your solutions won't be sustainable. When you hit on the root cause, you'll not only be able to address symptoms, you'll be prepared to meet any future challenges that come your way.

Now that you've determined your big-picture ideal or outcome, how do you turn that into an intent clear enough to guide yourself or your team's work? You use criteria.

SPECIFYING TYPES OF CRITERIA

When defining success for yourself or your team, you will need to create a list of criteria. You will have to sort and prioritize your criteria so it's obvious what is most important. Yet, a list by itself isn't useful. Telling someone forty features you want in your new house will get you nowhere. No one house will have them all.

A useful acronym to help with determining importance is MSCW.[23] (Pronounced "Moscow.")

- Must-Haves
- Should-Haves
- Could-Haves
- Won't-Haves

---

23   This is a tool from Agile project management intended to help make decisions about the scope of a project. We have found it tremendously helpful in decision-making directly. It is pronounced, "Moscow."

MUST-HAVES

These criteria are your nonnegotiables. If an option doesn't have these criteria, it should not be chosen. If you must have X, Y, and Z, a successful outcome cannot only have X and Z. Without Y, the option is unworkable. The must-haves will change how you prioritize and weigh your criteria.

Performance Management System Must-Haves: Ability to (1) conduct annual performance evaluations in a cloud-based system; (2) track one-on-one meeting dates and notes between managers and direct reports; (3) track employee goals and progress; and (4) document constructive feedback.

Every potential option should be weighed against your must-haves before any additional work is done. If it has the criteria, it can be added to a list of potentials. If it does not, it gets crossed off.

SHOULD-HAVES

These criteria are very important, and a successful end state should have most or all of them if possible. Still, it's possible to compromise on a few. None are a deal breaker.

If you're working with a team, communicating should-haves makes decision-making easier. They know these factors are important, but not crucial.

Performance Management System Should-Haves: Ability to recognize employees for a job well done and conduct employee engagement surveys.

COULD-HAVES

These criteria would be nice, but can easily be eliminated to get more important factors. (In many cases, you may wish to eliminate this list in favor of a shorter, clearer list for your decision driver(s).)

Performance Management System Could-Haves: Ability to integrate with Microsoft Teams instant messaging.

WON'T-HAVES

The "won't-have" criteria can be another way of stating that the criteria listed are out of scope or not applicable to the decision at hand.

Performance Management System Won't-Haves: Timesheets, pay statements, or company benefits (Learnit has different processes/systems for these).

STEP RECAP...

Before we move on, let's recap the most important elements and action items in this step.

STEP ONE: DEFINING SUCCESS

This step helps you define where the decision is going. It has two aspects: the Commander's Intent, and the description of what a successful outcome will look like.

Come up with an intent statement or problem statement and post it on the board for every meeting. Then, from that intent, you further define success. Think about where you want to end up. What will it look like after the decision is implemented? What does that vision tell us about the criteria of the decision and how best it should be achieved?

Communication in this step is essential. It will be the difference between a team that continues to move in the same direction and one that diverges and wastes weeks of work. When you make your intent clear at a high level, and when you define your vision and criteria, the decision process becomes stronger. The intent and criteria will focus you along the path, and when changes happen, they will teach you how to pivot.

WHAT'S NEXT?

It's helpful for the decision driver to know which criteria are most important. If they have a clear idea of what is most important to the decision-maker, they can research options and eliminate poor fits. They can also rank the remaining options realistically.

The decision driver can look at twenty options. If they have a clear picture of success, they will know what factors will be nonnegotiable, whether from the must-haves or won't-haves. That definition might eliminate fifteen of the options. The driver can then use the should-have criteria to choose one recommendation and one backup option. It will be easy for them to explain to you why they choose one over the other based on your criteria.

Without a clear definition of success, though, that work may or may not yield the results you're looking for.

Now that you or your decision driver have a clear idea of success, what is the next step? You'll need to gather information.

CHAPTER FIVE

STEP TWO

GATHER INFORMATION

INFORMATION CAN SAVE THE WORLD. (THAT'S WHY GOV-ernments employ spies!)

Take the work of Oleg Gordievsky, a Russian colonel who defected and spied for MI6, formerly known as the British Secret Intelligence Service, during the Cold War. The information that Gordievsky provided to MI6 was invaluable to Britain and its allies' efforts against the Soviet Union during the Cold War. It probably averted a nuclear war. You know, small potatoes.

Gordievsky was a double agent. On the British side, he shared information on the KGB and outed Russian-backed double agents in MI6. On the Russian side, he facilitated information sharing on Margaret Thatcher, Britain's leader at the time, to both Mikhail Gorbachev, the USSR leader at the time, *and* Margaret Thatcher herself to ensure that whenever they encountered each other at summits or other political events, Thatcher could always smoothly navigate their interactions.

Oddly enough, the information sharing was positive for both sides. The two leaders used the information to create a good working relationship.

Gordievsky also likely directly prevented a nuclear confrontation between Russia and the West. He learned that the Soviets were interpreting a NATO military exercise as a potential first strike against the KGB and were planning to retaliate. As a result, he lobbied hard to convince Thatcher and President Reagan to tone down the rhetoric around nuclear arms and to communicate the exercise clearly. The Russians reacted to the softening by averting the strikes.

Imagine the consequences if Gordievsky hadn't collected that information and the leaders of these countries had started a nuclear war. Worldwide devastation was prevented not through military force, but through the covert exchange of intelligence. *That's* the power of getting the right information to the right people.

Any decision you make is only as good as the quality of the information you have about it.

THE RIGHT INFORMATION

A well-thought-out decision is impossible without accurate and useful information. Without information, you can't accurately weigh your options. You won't be able to understand your circumstances or predict possible outcomes.

When it comes to gathering information, try to hit the sweet spot between too little information and too much. Too little information and you'll be shooting in the dark. The odds of regretting your decision later are high.

There is also such a thing as too much information (and we don't mean the oversharing of personal details). Analysis paralysis comes from wanting too much information before committing to a decision, and it inevitably leads to hoarding more and more information to the exclusion of action. Some personality types are more prone to analysis paralysis than others (for example, the C in the DiSC model, as precision and accuracy are extremely important to them), although every type can get stuck.

Someone who is more results oriented (such as the D type) may need to talk the issue through out loud. By giving themselves a timeframe to talk, and then a timeframe to act, they may be able to move forward more easily. For example, "I want to decide by noon tomorrow. I'll put together as many details as I can before then, but at noon, I will sit down and write up my decision and the assumptions that led to it."

There's a famous shareholder letter written by Jeff Bezos where he talks about his approach to decision-making. He says that while having all the information to make a decision would be nice, the reality is that waiting to decide until you know every detail is a recipe for disaster.

"Most decisions should probably be made with somewhere around 70 percent of the information you wish you had," Bezos wrote. "If you wait for 90 percent, in most cases, you're probably being slow." To avoid analysis paralysis, we recommend adopting Jeff Bezos's 70 percent rule. If you wait for perfect information, you'll wait too long.

Try to fill in as many of your blind spots as possible so that you can decide with confidence. What does the right information look like? That varies from case to case, but it's a good start to consider the following:

- Who are the stakeholders?
- Who are the experts?
- Have you done your due diligence?

CONSIDER STAKEHOLDERS

Who is involved in the decision-making process? Have you already designated the driver, decision-maker, and implementer roles? Have you collected all of the input needed from the people involved? Think through who will be impacted by the decision and ensure you understand the outcomes (positive and negative) each person could face as a result of your decision.

Many poor decisions come from failing to consider the impacts on a specific group. Fortunately, many results can be foreseen based on history. If you're new to an organization, check with people who've clocked more time in the organization to see if your ideas have been tried before. Not only can they provide valuable feedback, but they may also share some great solutions of their own.

For example, if you're considering changing your company's process for obtaining support from the IT Team, consider the different stakeholder groups and how issues will be prioritized. If someone is completely locked out of the company's network, does that take priority over an IT support ticket for someone who needs new software installed? Are there customer-facing employees who must be given immediate attention if a system goes down (e.g., cannot accept payment when trying to check out a customer)? How will the changes be communicated to stakeholders? How can you help them understand the benefits? Is there a feedback loop, if there are unforeseen consequences to the changes?

Scenario planning is critical, taking into account any stakeholders who will be impacted by a decision. There are multiple angles to every situation, and it's important for you as a decision-maker to take them all into account. Don't just scratch the surface. Involve many stakeholders in the decision-making process.

FIND EXPERTS

Even if you're already an expert in the subject matter of the decision, it is always a good idea to research best practices and standards. Has this problem been solved before, either inside or outside your industry?

Everyone has blind spots. We recommend consulting other people who are experts on the subject and who can expand your knowledge. Many times, other organizations in your industry will have solved the problem you face, and you can learn from their experience. Alternatively, consider finding groups outside of your organization who have solved problems that may lend themselves to similar solutions. For example, when exploring options for a new IT ticketing system, you may want to contact a consulting company and inquire about how others in your industry are thriving in this area. Why create processes from scratch when others have already successfully cracked the code? Consult subject matter experts on the topic of your problem from several angles. You may be able to find them through research associations that look into best practices.

When you're researching how peers have handled similar problems and decisions, look first at organizations similar to yours. If you're making business decisions for a small startup, it's best not to use the outcomes of large enterprises as a benchmark, even if the rest of the situation is similar. Scale is a major factor in the effectiveness of a decision. The best peer information comes from businesses that are in the same category as yours in terms of operation and budget size. (Be sure to look outside your industry too.)

For example, when Damon was looking to roll out a subscription model for learning software, he looked into the subscription rollout for Peloton, among others. Yes, it was a completely different product, but the scale and model were similar enough to provide valuable insight.

You can also apply this concept on an operational level. Even though Learnit is not in the health and wellness industry, Damon has gotten valuable insight into subscription models by purchasing a Peloton and subscribing to the monthly services, truly understanding the customer's perspective. When gathering information, it doesn't always have to be apples to apples. Get creative and learn how to adapt successful business models from other industries and fields. He then went back to Learnit and adapted some of their passion-centered approaches to customer service to Learnit's needs. Look for learning experiences in all that you do. You never know what's going to cross over and lead to better results in the future.

Don't assume you need to reinvent the wheel. If you can find someone who has solved this problem or one like it before, you will save a huge amount of time and effort. It's better to be a learn-it-all than a know-it-all.

STUDY PAST DECISIONS

Take a look at your organization's past decisions. What can you learn about what works from previous projects? As the adage goes: history will repeat itself if you don't learn from it. Take the time to comb through any data to spot past mistakes. Where were the failures, and what can you do to avoid repeating them?

Leverage the experience of others wherever you can. No matter how well-versed you are in a subject, there's always more to learn. Look for opportunities to expand your options and awareness, and to identify risk early. Smart research now will lead to amazing solutions and decreased risk later.

DOING DUE DILIGENCE

Complexity varies across decisions. If the situation you're considering is more complex, return to your criteria for success and your future vision now. What research is most important? (This will likely be related to your "must-haves.") Have you accounted for how your criteria interact? Have you discussed the possible decision options with stakeholders and experts as needed?

Perhaps most importantly, have you ensured you're using the *right* information?

DETERMINING QUALITY INFORMATION

Not all information is good quality information, and it's important to be discerning. Ensure you're using sources that are relevant, trustworthy, and current.

That being said, you don't want to just go with the first set of information you happen across. Seek out information and get creative with your methods for acquiring it. You can even buy information online from resources like digital research journals and data brokers that can be useful to you in the right context.

For example, if a doctor tells you that the only solution to lowering your blood pressure is to take a certain prescription, don't just take the doctor's word for it. The doctor could be right, but they could also be mistaken. Get a second opinion. Also, seek out advice from other people who have successfully controlled their high blood pressure. Consider paying to read articles about blood pressure published in medical journals. Avoid relying on a single source, even if it's a good one. A wide variety of perspectives will always lead to the best understanding.

Be sure to verify your sources. Fact-check and use up-to-date information. Especially with the internet, there is an abundance of data at your fingertips, but not all of it is good. Look for credible and current information from reputable people and organizations. Consult peer-reviewed research, recent or respected published books and biographies, international data (especially if you're in a global organization), and specialized associations when you can. Look for respected people rather than just anyone.

Validating information is especially important with artificial intelligence, such as ChatGPT. ChatGPT is a large language model developed by OpenAI that uses the GPT (Generative Pre-trained Transformer) architecture. GPT is a neural network architecture that uses self-attention mechanisms to process input data, and it has been trained on a massive amount of text data from the internet to generate human-like responses to input text. To generate its responses, ChatGPT uses a technique called unsupervised learning, which means that it is not explicitly told what to say, but rather learns to generate responses based on the text data it is trained on. This allows it to be flexible and adaptable, and to generate responses that are appropriate for a wide range of conversations. So, guess what? ChatGPT isn't always accurate!

Don't just rely on ChatGPT or Google and reference sources that support your ideas, and be mindful not to fall prey to confirmation bias. This is why it's good to pay for access to resources that can provide reliable benchmarks rather than only using free or open-access resources. Be sure to consult experts and sources with a variety of perspectives, to round out your understanding.

For example, if you're looking to hire a candidate for a new position in your company, it's a good idea to pay for a service that provides benchmarks for salary data in that industry, position level, and location. This information is worth paying for because otherwise, you risk making an offer that is under market value without even realizing it. You might lose a candidate you wanted—or overpay that candidate and lose money on your new hire.

Another good strategy for avoiding confirmation bias is documenting your assumptions at the beginning of this process and referencing them as you learn more. Have you found at least one major piece of information from a good source that challenges your initial assumptions? If not, keep looking until you do.

WHEN GOOD INFORMATION IS HARD TO FIND

Documenting your assumptions is always worth doing. For example, if you're deciding on a location for a residential real estate building project, what do you assume the building materials will cost? If material costs are significantly different from what you thought, it may change your cost-benefit ratio and impact your decision (or at least your strategy for implementing the decision). If an assumption will impact the results of your decision, it's important to research it early. It may drive possible options later.

If you can't find great information to inform the decision you're considering, your options are to operate on your assumptions (which you should also stress test!) and hope for the best outcome, or slow down and hold off on deciding until you can get better information. Obviously the latter puts this stage on pause for the time being, which may lose you opportunities.

This is why decision-making is hard and messy. You will never have all the time and information you need.

If you choose to move forward with the decision despite the lack of information, one way to make up for it is to pilot at a small scale. For example, during the COVID-19 lockdowns, there was no reliable information about when people could safely return to the office. No one knew when another wave of outbreaks or variants would arise. What you don't know, you can often pilot. A particular company decided to use a small-scale pilot to gather the information needed. They returned a single branch to onsite operations. After a few months, they had built up good information about what logistics and challenges had arisen. They surveyed the affected employees and addressed their concerns before deciding to bring everyone back or to continue remotely. Choosing a small-scale pilot allows you to make a larger-scale decision freely, while learning from the experience, without having to backtrack.

Piloting at a small scale generates data to make better-informed decisions at full scale.

QUANTITATIVE VERSUS QUALITATIVE DATA

Data is critical to making objective decisions. It's important when collecting data or information that you do not just focus on numbers. Yes, quantitative (number-based) data is important, and you should collect some. Qualitative data, which is based on more subjective data, like opinion surveys and written comments, is also a valuable window into the needs and landmines of a particular decision type.

Both people and technical considerations should matter in any decision. This is an opportunity to practice the self-awareness we talked about in Chapter Two, and to deliberately expand your thinking beyond your natural personality type. Whether you're a thinker drawn to quantitative data or a feeler drawn to qualitative data, make sure you have a good understanding of both the numbers and the human impact of your decisions.

Qualitative Data Examples	Quantitative Data Examples
• Texts	• Metrics
• Documents	• Measurements
• Audio recordings	• Counters
• Video recordings	• Tests & experiments
• Images	• Surveys
• Symbols	• Projections
• Interview transcripts	• Market reports

DOUBLE-CHECK YOUR MOTIVATION

If you're gathering information because you're afraid of making the wrong decision, gathering endless data almost certainly won't alleviate your fear. It's natural to worry about making the wrong decision, but be mindful of your motivations. Avoid the analysis-paralysis trap.

Spend some time gathering a reasonable amount of due diligence. Then figure out the worst-case scenario and consider how you will deal with it. If you're still experiencing anxiety about this decision after both of those exercises, then it's time to go back into the psychology behind your decision-making. You may have to address your fear in another way or move forward despite the fear, trusting yourself to have done what you should.

STEP RECAP...

Before we move on, let's recap the most important elements and action items in this step.

STEP TWO: GATHERING INFORMATION

Good decisions come from good input.

It's critical to get not only information but the right information. The challenge of decision-making in the modern era is that there's so much information to sift through. That's why this step focuses on curating and processing details.

The driver of the decision does not have to be an expert on the specifics of the decision. They do need to know what experts to include on the team to provide input. They should also balance the need to keep the decision moving with the need to accurately assess risk and fill blind spots.

Either the driver of the decision or the influencers can do research, but every person involved in this step must curate carefully. Again, use your self-awareness here to leverage your strengths and compensate for your weaknesses. Many of the worst decisions came about because a decision-maker or driver assumed they were an expert when in fact they were not. Or, they didn't validate the information they used to make the decision. Lean on the expertise of the people you work with, and allow their wisdom and real-world experience to inform you.

WHAT'S NEXT?

The right information can be the difference between success and failure. As Donald Rumsfeld aptly said, "There are known knowns; there are things we know we know. We also know there are known unknowns; that is to say, we know there are some things we do not know. But there are also unknown unknowns—the ones we don't know we don't know."

In this chapter, we illustrated how relevant, trustworthy, and up-to-date information is vital to the decision-making process. We pointed to several strategies for gathering this information. Start by documenting your assumptions, then conduct your research. When in doubt, find and consult experts. Be sure to consider all the angles of your decisions, including the numbers and the opinions of the people your decisions impact.

Now that you've assembled good information at the level of detail you need for all the pieces of your decision, go back to your intent. The next step is to use what you've learned to determine the best path forward by creating a list of possible decision options. To do that well, you'll need to keep in mind why you're making the decision to begin with.

CHAPTER SIX

STEP THREE

OUTLINE POSSIBLE OPTIONS

WHEN IT COMES TO WEIGHING OPTIONS, MANY PEOPLE tend to fall into the trap of a false binary. As we discussed in Chapter One, this is when you turn situations into either-or choices. In almost every case, the best solution is a third path that wasn't immediately obvious.

Take the decision Damon had to make at the end of his senior year of high school in 1990. While preparing to graduate, he received an offer to play professional baseball in the minor leagues. At the time, it seemed like Damon had two choices before him: accept the offer and play for the minor league Atlanta Braves, or follow his original plan and attend university to play at the collegiate level while earning a degree.

Damon had long dreamed of becoming a professional baseball player, but he'd never expected the chance to arrive so soon. He didn't feel ready at seventeen to travel the country with a team of twenty-something-year-old players. On the other hand, he knew if he declined and went to university as planned, it would be at least three years before he'd get another chance to go pro.

In the end, Damon declined the offer and attended a four-year university. Though he's happy with the way his life turned out, in hindsight, he overlooked a third option. He could have found the middle ground. Because baseball was more important to him than school back then, it might have been better for Damon to attend a junior college rather than a four-year university to play collegiate baseball. This would have allowed him more time to hone his skills and gain some life experience outside of high school before trying out for the minor league.

Damon ultimately did play for a minor league team, but his path to getting there was temporarily derailed because he decided to attend university. Perhaps if he had made a list of all the possible paths to achieving his career goal, he would have seen the better middle path.

The good news is, while the false binary trap is easy to fall into, the key to dodging it is *also* easy. You simply need to brainstorm and create a list of possible options.

BRAINSTORMING BEST PRACTICES

Brainstorming every possible option is an important part of doing your due diligence. It helps you consider *all* the possibilities rather than just the two most obvious ones. It's an important—and often overlooked—step of the decision-making process.

By being creative at this step, you open doors that may lead to profoundly better decisions. Like Damon, there may be another option you have not considered that gives you all the outcomes you want.

DON'T BRAINSTORM ALONE

In the last step, you should have invited and considered the input of all critical parties. This includes the stakeholders (input), the driver, the decision-maker(s), and the implementer. It likely included experts on the topic as well. Those conversations may naturally have led to decision options. If so, take this time to document those options.

Then, brainstorm all possible options. We're saying "all," and we mean *all*.

This should be done while including more than one perspective. Even if the decision is on a personal matter that only affects you, brainstorm with a trusted friend or family member. If you're the driver of a business or personal decision that affects more than just you, include the others impacted in brainstorming. Include one subject-matter expert on a critical part of the decision. Be strategic. A group will come up with more options than just a single person, and that's almost always to the benefit of the decision. (Again, the right answer is likely not in the first couple of ideas you have considered.)

We recommend talking potential options through with as many people as practical. It's a good idea to brainstorm with at minimum one trusted colleague outside of the people already consulted, even if your colleague is not directly impacted by the decision. Ideally, this colleague will be able to spot risks early on based on their knowledge or ability with logic and questions. It's also helpful to invite at least one subject-matter expert to your brainstorming session.

PLANT THE SEED BEFOREHAND

Rather than starting the brainstorming session cold, let people know in advance that you want them to bring ideas to the table.

In our own teams, we typically ask everyone to come to the meeting with three ideas written on sticky notes (more on that later). This gets everyone thinking about solutions and broadens the scope of possibilities before brainstorming even begins.

Advanced preparation encourages everyone to smoothly transition into building on each other's ideas. This is the heart of a good ideation session and will increase the odds of your group landing on the best solution.

ENSURE EVERYONE IS HEARD

Requesting input from stakeholders (including subject-matter experts), drivers, decision-makers, and implementers, can quickly lead to brainstorming with a large group. That can become chaotic and unproductive if there are no ground rules. This is why we suggest also including a facilitator in brainstorming meetings. Facilitators don't have an emotional investment in the outcome, so they are great at keeping people on task, calling for breaks and holding people accountable for their behavior when emotions run high, and making sure everyone's voice is heard (even the quiet introverts). They keep the process moving smoothly.

If you choose not to involve a facilitator in your meeting, another strategy for ensuring all voices are heard is going around the room. Take turns and set time limits for everyone to speak. Without actively making space for them to be heard, introverts are not likely to speak up. Everyone in a brainstorming session should be there for a reason. If only extroverts get all the floor time, you're losing the value of having a diversity of voices in the first place.

LEADERS SPEAK LAST

When the leader is first to voice their ideas in brainstorming, you may be fanning the flames of groupthink. People may not be willing to challenge the leader and risk upsetting them by pointing out issues. When people aren't willing to speak up, creativity is suppressed, accountability disappears, and the best ideas never happen. We've seen firsthand that when a leader voices their ideas first, it effectively turns the rest of the team into yes people, often leading right back to the binary thinking you were trying to escape in the first place.

Groupthink is also problematic because it's disingenuous, which can often lead to poor decisions. In addition, research shows that pressure to compromise workplace ethics is on the rise. According to the 2021 *Global Business Ethics Survey Report*, "30 percent of US employees agreed that they experienced pressure to compromise their organization's workplace ethics standards, a 14 percentage point increase since 2017."[24] This is part of an ongoing trend; pressure has consistently increased over the last decade. Some of the double-digit increase in pressure between 2017 and 2020 was likely due to the COVID-19 pandemic. That's the last thing you want for your organization.

When it comes to ethics, the buck always stops at the leader. If you're in a leadership position, you need to set an example. Be on the lookout for gray areas in your company's ethics standards and practices. Avoid the murky compliance that results from groupthink.

Thankfully, groupthink is easy to avoid. The leader should

---

24 *2021 Global Business Ethics Survey Report: The State of Ethics & Compliance in the Workplace, a Look at Global Trends* (Vienna, VA: Ethics & Compliance Initiative, March 2021), 13, https://www. ethics.org/wp-content/uploads/2021-ECI-GBES-State-Ethics-Compliance-in-Workplace.pdf.

be last to voice their ideas and opinions. That way everyone will feel more comfortable sharing what comes to mind. Positive feedback from the leader can also work wonders to reinforce this sense of security, leading to better brainstorming and, ultimately, a better decision.

DON'T CAST JUDGMENT

There is no room for judgment in effective brainstorming! At this stage, no possible solution or action should be left out, even the most outrageous of ideas—in fact, oftentimes the crazy ideas inspire others that ultimately lead to your best solution.

The only bad ideas are the ones left unsaid.

If you start rejecting ideas, people will get discouraged and shut down. You don't want to cut off the creative pipeline by getting critical too early, so don't judge or reject any idea yet. Just get as many in the air—or on the board—as possible.

The best action you can take at the brainstorming stage is to change your mindset from "yes, but..." to "yes and...." You might be surprised at the difference this simple change makes.

CREATE A VISUAL AID

Visual aids support more than just visual thinkers. For ideas, a visual aid is a great equalizer. We suggest using a whiteboard and sticky notes. If every idea is written on a sticky note, it's easy to rearrange as you look for patterns, create categories, or combine ideas. This makes it easier to slap every idea that comes to mind on the board *before* digging deep to determine the most viable and effective ones (more on that in Chapter Seven).

To optimize facilitation and communication, we strongly

encourage conducting brainstorming sessions in person. Being able to see and interpret your colleagues' body language is an underrated element of productive discussions. Positive energy happens *in the room*. As your team is working together and exchanging ideas, this kind of "good vibe" can keep the process motoring along. However, since teams are becoming increasingly global, in-person meetings are not always possible.

If you can't conduct your brainstorming session in person, the visual aid is even more crucial. Use visual collaboration software like Miro to create a virtual whiteboard with sticky notes so that everyone can contribute, the same as in a conference room. You will still get the value of multiple people contributing to the list of possible options on the whiteboard, which is the most important element of this stage. All the same rules apply: type whatever ideas come to mind and throw them on the board on a sticky note. It's also important not to cast judgment, have the leader speak last, etc. Also, we highly encourage asking participants to turn their cameras on, so you can keep an eye on body language during the brainstorming session.

To further support visual thinkers and get the best use out of your visual aid, we suggest grouping your whiteboard stickies into an affinity diagram (see Chapter Four) before you enter the narrowing phase of the decision-making process.

ASSUME POSITIVE INTENT

Brainstorming as a group is great, but let's not pretend...it can also come with difficulties. Every group has at least one unwelcome devil's advocate. They get critical too early in the process and inadvertently block creativity, stopping the flow of idea generation.

Clashing personality types and tendencies can also cause conflict during brainstorming, especially if your team is discussing a high-stakes, high-impact decision. To help mitigate this, remind everyone to *assume positive intent* whenever a team member presents an idea or gives feedback.

Assume they mean well. Assume their ideas are genuine—maybe even helpful—but possibly just poorly expressed. It will help you to keep your own emotional reactions in check and allow you to listen for insights you might otherwise miss.

This is another reason we suggest including a facilitator in these discussions. If the facilitator is made aware of certain personalities to look out for, they can be better equipped to reel an enthusiastic devil's advocate or dominating extrovert back in. They can ensure the idea-generation process is not disrupted or corrupted by emotions.

You can help yourself out by setting expectations at the start of your brainstorming session. Create an agenda detailing the purpose and process of the meeting, including when you'll be open to criticism in the next step. This allows your team members to note their concerns and questions about ideas, but save them for the narrowing process.

STEP RECAP...

Before we move on, let's recap the most important elements and action items in this step.

STEP THREE: CREATING A LIST OF POSSIBLE OPTIONS

There are nearly always more choices than the binary yes or no, on-or-off decisions. In this step, you'll find them.

Work to widen your potential choices, being as creative as

possible. Brainstorm without judgment. Make the list long, and be creative. If you're working with a team, be sure to set up the problem you're brainstorming. Make it clear to everyone in the meeting that you're not shooting down ideas. (Any idea is a great idea because any idea might lead to the *right* idea.) Encourage people to share their ideas, and specifically ask for input from introverts.

To get the best results, it helps to be proactive. Give people direction and assign prework before the meeting. It will tend to make the process more efficient, leading to better brainstorming and better discussion.

WHAT'S NEXT?

It's rare that you ever have to make a decision based only on two choices. If you find yourself thinking, *This or that,* it's probably time to brainstorm. Otherwise, you may fall into binary thinking and miss the best option entirely. The perfect answer almost always hides behind the obvious ones.

Once you're ready to wrap up the idea generation part of the decision-making process, compile your ideas into a list. In the next step, you will refine and narrow the list until you have a small number of great options to choose from.

Keep reading to learn how to narrow it.

CHAPTER SEVEN

STEP FOUR

NARROW IT DOWN

KANDIS'S SISTER, KATE, WAS STRUGGLING WITH A DECI-sion.

She was trying to decide what city to move to after spending several years in South America, but the decision had become murky and emotional. Instead of feeling excited about moving to a new location, she was second-guessing herself every step of the way. She was deciding among several cities: Kansas City, Missouri; Cleveland, Ohio; San Francisco, California; and Reno, Nevada. She assembled her list of criteria. She wanted to live in a place where she could walk to a restaurant. The city had to be affordable, enough so that she could purchase a home that fit her needs. She needed to be able to find a job that she enjoyed in the hospitality industry. She also had her "wish list." There were some city "vibes" she preferred, kinds of cultural experiences, and types of community. The biggest item on her mind though, was family. Of both the four-legged and humankind.

Kate has two dogs. It was important to her that there be

a dog park close to where she lived. A fenced yard would be necessary too. She wanted to be in a dog-friendly neighborhood. She wanted to be in a place where walks would be plentiful and restaurants might offer bowls of water for thirsty four-legged friends on occasion. She wanted her dogs to have room to roam and the opportunity to be cooed at by other dog-loving neighbors.

Her family lived around Kansas City, and that was a major draw. She didn't know how heavily to weigh that criterion, though. She worried she was only considering Kansas because of the pull of her family. She wanted to be close, but she didn't want to compromise other high-priority items in service of proximity. Living next to an airport was critical, so as long as she could take a direct flight to Kansas City, that would give her access to family. Was she placing too much weight on this criteria, over the other criteria on her list? Would one of those be more important?

When approaching a big decision, it's not uncommon to find yourself facing a too-long list of criteria. A wish list can grow unchecked and without a system for sorting, weighting, and ultimately narrowing down criteria—actually making the decision can feel nearly impossible.

There are different kinds of criteria, and there are criteria of different weights. Once you have your list of criteria, begin breaking them down. This is a great time to put the MSCW acronym to use. Separate your criteria into Must-have, Should-have, Could-have, and Won't-have. It will immediately give you a clear picture of how you're thinking about priorities.

Must-haves are a great place to start. Your must-haves are your nonnegotiables. They are the criteria without which you will walk away. No deal. Must-haves give important clues to what you consider a successful outcome. If you know your must-haves are X, Y, and Z, then your successful outcome will contain X, Y, and Z. Knowing this will help you prioritize and, as you begin to narrow, will help you to weight criteria.

For Kandis's sister, this was a complicated, high-impact decision. She knew that being close to family was important, and she had other big-ticket items on her list as well.

Whether it's a personal or a high-impact decision moment for your organization, the ultimate goal in narrowing the field is always the same. *What's most important?* What is most important to your organization? What is the end goal of the initiative and do the criteria reflect that? In a high-impact decision, there might be a long list of items that are "important" but starting from your success criteria and working backward to narrow your choices will go a long way to helping you start to narrow.

Ultimately, Kandis's sister did move to Kansas City. It was the right decision, for many reasons. We'll talk about how she got there, and the tools she used to help, a little later in the chapter.

THE CHALLENGE OF NARROWING

It is hard to narrow.

We know it. We've seen it. We've experienced it.

You need to narrow to avoid binary decisions. You don't want to be choosing only between two options. You also don't want to have fifty options on the table when there are multiple decision-makers in the process. Otherwise, you're going to have ten different people pulling in ten different directions. Narrowing a group decision is more challenging than combing through your own list of house-buying must-haves, but no less important. A too-long list of criteria is going to create a stalemate in any kind of group decision-making process. Remember that your goal is making your way toward that successful decision-making end state.

For all these reasons, narrowing is a critical early step. It's also hard. You'll be forced to eliminate options that seem perfectly suitable. People will be strongly attached to some of them. Emotions will flare. Egos will rear their heads. People will defend their ideas aggressively, and you will need strategies for how to counteract upset or prevent it before it starts. Prevention begins with planning.

Even in the toughest boardrooms in the world, people have anxiety. High-impact decisions, in particular, bring up a lot of fear. People want to get it right. Sometimes they want to get it right so much, they'd rather avoid the decision than make the wrong one.

As a side note: if that's you—if there's fear in the room or your heart when you're working toward a big decision—we've found that the best remedy is also the most readily available—time. Allow some time to process and think. Don't compare your thought process to anyone else's. Don't rush yourself to be ready before you are. No one expects you to be able to brainstorm and narrow down the dozens of ideas that brainstorming elicited, in the very same meeting. Take one session to brainstorm, let everyone recharge, and plan another session for narrowing down ideas. Decision fatigue is real and it can start very early in the process. Einstein always said his best ideas came to him in the shower, or on a walk. They always came in the moments his mind wasn't feeling the crunch of *I must know the answer*! Give yourself the gift of a moment to walk away. If it was good for Einstein, it's good enough for you.

When Kandis is leading client groups through the decision-making process, she often has them brainstorm on day one and narrow down on day two. That little gap of time allows people to get grounded, putting distance between their emotions and the task at hand. It allows people who need time to process that freedom. It's also always better to be well-rested before narrowing options.

WHY NOT "PROS AND CONS?"

A pros and cons list isn't the right tool for high-impact decisions. Pros and cons have no weight. The implicit test in the pros and cons list is to count: more pros, you say yes, more cons, you say no. Counting leaves a lot of gray areas. Your pros list might overshadow your cons list, from a numbers perspective, but what if the few cons on your list are the most important criteria for your decision? You need a system for weighing your options so that you can compare them in a more nuanced way. Your goal should be elimination. You don't need to rush to a decision based on which "column" contains more items.

Your goal is to move away from "good" and "bad" and ask yourself, "What criteria am I going to use to make this decision?"

For Kandis's sister, being able to walk to a restaurant was more important to her than having a fenced backyard, as she could always pay someone to install a fence. She also knew that she needed to live within a short drive to an airport, based on her lifestyle. It requires critical thinking to narrow your options.

WEIGHING CRITERIA

Simply said: criteria help you boil down what matters most. Making good decisions is ultimately about making decisions based on what's *important* to you...not just whatever is in front of you.

Criteria are what ground us. They are what allow us to describe in detail what's most important in that successful end state. Of course, you're not going to worry so much about the complexities of criteria when you're trying to decide what to have for dinner. That's a low-impact decision, and you're going to have some concerned family members if you break out a decision-making matrix every time you have to answer, "Pizza or meatloaf?" The processes we're going to outline are most useful for what we call "high-impact decisions."

Let's say we're looking to open a factory in a new state, one we haven't done business in before, and we know there are going to be many hugely important criteria: What are the taxes in that state? What's the cost of doing business there? Are there readily available workers that we can hire for this plant? Will this factory be a welcome addition to the community or will there be resistance? Are there enough housing options to support the number of people and their families who will work in the factory? (This is especially important in rural areas!) These criteria impact the success of the factory and the reputation of the company. They carry a lot of weight.

Deciding criteria can happen in various ways. Sometimes the decision-maker declares, "Here's what's important." Sometimes criteria come from an organizational or strategic plan. To align your decisions with your organization, you need to know what the organization values. Often these values are contained within a five-year strategic plan. Criteria should reflect core values and the original intent of your project.

DECISION-MAKING MATRIX

A decision-making matrix can be valuable when making high-impact decisions. A decision-making matrix with weighted criteria is a tool that helps to evaluate and compare options based on a set of criteria that are considered important to the decision-maker. It involves assigning weights to each criterion to reflect its relative importance, and then evaluating each option based on how well it satisfies each criterion.

Buying a House: Decision-Making Criteria

Must Have

- Within one mile of restaurants (walkable)
- Be within budget: not to exceed $XXX,XXX
- Within fifteen miles of airport

Should Have

- Be able to visit family in Kansas City within six hours (flight/car)
- Within five miles of a dog park
- A fenced backyard
- Option for gas stove
- Fireplace

Could Have

- Up to $9,000 work required on house to meet needs

Won't Have

- Townhouse or condo
- More than $10,000 work required to meet needs

These matrices come in all shapes and sizes, and there is no wrong way to approach one, as long as you know the fundamental components and your end goal. Designing a matrix that is not binary is key. Don't put yourself in a position to decide between only two options.

Let's take a look at a sample matrix with options for buying specific houses in the cities that Kate was considering.

Step 1

Enter a list of options/solutions you wish to evaluate and you will ultimately rank in priority order.

Options/Solutions
Kansas City - House 1
Kansas City - House 2
Kansas City - House 3
San Francisco - House 1
San Francisco - House 2
San Francisco - House 3
Reno - House 1
Reno - House 2
Cleveland - House 1
Cleveland - House 2

Step 2

List the Evaluation Criteria each option will be evaluated against.

	Evaluation Criteria
#1	Within one mile of restaurants (walkable)
#2	Within budget: not to exceed $XXX,XXX
#3	Within fifteen miles of airport
#4	Able to visit family in MO within six hours (flight/car)
#5	Within five miles of a dog park
#6	A fenced backyard
#7	Jobs available in hospitality industry
#8	Up to $X,XXX work required on house to meet needs

Step 3

Give each Evaluation Criterion a weight using the scale provided. This is used to calculate a total score and priority rank of options.

	Evaluation Criteria	Weight of Criteria
#1	Within one mile of restaurants (walkable)	3
#2	Within budget: not to exceed $XXX,XXX	3
#3	Within fifteen miles of airport	3
#4	Able to visit family in MO within six hours (flight/car)	2
#5	Within five miles of a dog park	2
#6	A fenced backyard	2
#7	Jobs available in hospitality industry	2
#8	Up to $X,XXX work required on house to meet needs	1

Weight Scale: 3 - *Significantly More Important,* **2** - *More Important,* **1** - *Important*

How to use a decision-making matrix:

1. Identify the decision to be made and the options or solutions that are available. Tip: Only add options and solutions to the matrix that meet all "Must-Have" criteria.
2. Determine the criteria that are relevant to the decision. These should be factors that are important to the decision-maker and can be used to objectively evaluate the options and solutions.
3. Assign weights to each criterion to reflect its relative importance (we used 1 = important; 2 = more important; and 3 = significantly more important).
4. Create a matrix with the options listed on the left-hand side and the criteria listed at the top.
5. Evaluate each option or solution against each criterion and rate them in alignment with the evaluation scale (0 = strongly disagree; 1 = disagree; 2 = neither agree nor disagree; 3 = agree; and 4 = strongly agree).
6. Multiply each rating by the weight of the corresponding criterion to obtain a weighted score for each option. (We used Excel calculations to help us with this step, which is not pictured.)
7. Sum the weighted scores for each option or solution to obtain the total score.
8. Put the options in priority order, with the highest score at the top of the list, meaning that option best meets the criteria.

Step 4

List all options/solutions down the left-hand side of a matrix and the criteria along the top.

Step 5

Evaluate and score each option/solution against each criterion using the Evaluation Scale of 0-4.

Options/Solutions	Evaluation Criteria							
	#1	#2	#3	#4	#5	#6	#7	#8
Kansas City - House 1	4	4	3	4	4	4	3	2
Kansas City - House 2	2	3	3	4	4	4	3	2
Kansas City - House 3	3	1	3	4	2	2	3	2
San Francisco - House 1	4	1	3	3	2	1	3	2
San Francisco - House 2	3	1	3	3	2	1	3	2
San Francisco - House 3	3	1	3	3	2	1	3	2
Reno - House 1	1	2	4	2	3	4	4	2
Reno - House 2	3	2	4	2	3	4	4	2
Cleveland - House 1	3	3	3	2	2	2	3	3
Cleveland - House 2	2	3	3	2	1	2	3	3

Evaluation Scale: 4 - Strongly Agree, **3** - Agree, **2** - Neither Agree Nor Disagree, **1** - Disagree, **0** - Strongly Disagree

Step 6

Multiply each rating by the weight of the corresponding criterion to obtain a weighted score for each option. (We used Excel calculations to help us with this step, which is not pictured.)

Step 7

Sum the weighted scores for each option or solution to obtain the total score.

Step 8

Put the options in priority order, with the highest score at the top of the list, meaning that option best meets the criteria.

Options/Solutions	Total Evaluation Score
Kansas City - House 1	65
Kansas City - House 2	56
Reno - House 2	55
Reno - House 1	49
Cleveland - House 1	48
Kansas City - House 3	45
San Francisco - House 1	44
Cleveland - House 2	43
San Francisco - House 2	41
San Francisco - House 3	41

When creating the matrix, it's up to you what your evaluation criteria look like and how much weight you give to each. You might only have your "significantly more important" criteria on the matrix. Their weights might be similar and can support you in determining which option *best* meets the intent of the decision. You might have a combination of "significantly more important," "more important," and "important" criteria with varied weights. Even the design of the matrix and the process of choosing criteria help you start to narrow down your options. Again, we recommend leaving an option off of the matrix entirely if it doesn't meet all of your must-haves. The important job is to separate your options from your evaluation criteria.

This is an individual example, but a decision-making matrix can easily be used by stakeholders at work as well. The key is to decide on the options and criteria as a team and then ask each stakeholder to objectively rate each option against each criterion, ultimately giving each option a score. If stakeholders complete the matrix individually, one option is to then average the scores of each option and narrow it down to your best choice, your backup option, and your second backup. Then you can present those to the decision-makers. The matrix takes ill-fit options off the table, immediately. A matrix will ignite your critical thinking and short-circuit impulsivity based on emotions.

A decision-making matrix is also a valuable tool to cut through emotions. Feelings often crowd your ability to make a decision. Take the time to organize your criteria into "buckets" of must-have, should-have, could-have, and won't-have. Create a matrix and weigh each criterion in comparison to your options. Don't be afraid to take options off the table entirely.

BUY IN ON THE MATRIX

It's important, when presenting the decision-making matrix as a tool to a group of decision-makers, that you paint a clear picture of both the process and the end goal.

Before you start trying to eliminate options, make sure everyone understands the ranking systems. Agree on the intent of the matrix based on your decision goals. Make it clear that you're all going to decide together what the criteria are and how you'll weight them. Otherwise, it's going to feel to them like the rules are changing as you go. This kind of uncertainty eats away at trust.

Decision-makers, even those who come in with strong opinions, will yield to the matrix. Once you've walked them through the process, they'll see that it is truly an objective approach. They may come in with doubts, but you will be leading them through a process that feels fair, and by the end, they will have no choice but to come on board.

Lay out your process, generate the buy-in, and then narrow it. If you act in that order, you'll save substantial headaches down the road.

Please keep in mind, however, that a decision-making matrix is best used for high-impact, complex decisions. Several other tools are appropriate for making decisions of less complexity or impact.

COMPARING TO CONSTRAINTS

Before we put options into the decision-making matrix, we need to cross-check them with constraints that may exist.

There are many kinds of constraints: time, cost/resource, level of effort needed to complete a project, and potential risks involved in the implementation. Comparing your options to existing constraints means if you have a budget of $50,000 (constraint) and the cost to execute a particular option is $3 million...that isn't going to work.

You need to know your constraints. You could have a promising solution, but if it's going to cost three times more than your budget, it can't go in your list of options. Don't think of constraints as limitations. They are a great tool for eliminating unsuitable options. Identify your constraints early and refer to them often as you are narrowing down your options.

Time Constraint

A time constraint is just what it sounds like. *We absolutely have to have this solution implemented by December 1 and there is zero wiggle room.* That's a clear constraint. Can this option that you've brainstormed be implemented by December 1? If not, it's off the list.

Cost/Resource Constraints

The biggest resource constraint is usually budget. How much money do you have to invest to implement this decision?

Materials are another kind of resource constraint to consider. The availability (and speed) with which you can get materials or machinery that you need matters to whether you can implement the solution. Maybe you need to rent a piece of heavy equipment for one of the options. Compare that to your constraint. *Is this realistic?*

Level of Effort

Are you in an organization where people are already maxed out in their day-to-day at work? Do you have enough internal resources to successfully execute the decision in terms of person-hours and skillsets? If you don't, you'll need to determine where you intend to get them from. If you need to hire consultants or contractors, that's an additional monetary cost. If the team is maxed out and you don't have the budget to spend to bring in external resources, then the options with a heavy lift may need to come off the table.

RISK AND OTHER CONSIDERATIONS

Different options carry different levels of risk. Oftentimes, the needs of your organization will determine whether an option is a high, medium, or low risk. A high-risk option could cost the organization, for example, $50,000 to recover from. Or it might put the organization's reputation at risk. Reputation is another kind of risk (and some would argue, much higher than a simple loss of time and money.) Every organization, and sometimes different teams within the organization, is going to define risk in a slightly different way. That should be left to the decision-makers in question.

For our purposes, let's define risk as an event in the future that may or may not happen. If it does happen, it will impact your actual decision or a project that arises because of the decision. Risk can be either positive or negative.

Risk management within an organization means planning for outcomes that could negatively impact the organization, project, or decision. Start thinking about risk early. The earlier you get a clear idea of your risks, the more opportunities you will have to try and manage those risks through mitigation. Take specific actions to try and reduce the probability of a given risk occurring, or to reduce the impact if it does occur.

The impact of risk will vary: it may affect time, cost, or morale. If there is an associated cost risk, are you able to build in those necessary contingencies to keep the project on track? If the impact will be on company morale or employee engagement, can you put some plans in place to prepare your employees? Are you able to support them if the worst case plays out?

In all these scenarios, you'll need to think through what each risk, and its associated impacts, might look and feel like. If you continue to move in that direction, you'll need to plan for mitigation.

THE NEED FOR RESEARCH

Do your research to know where each option falls in the categories of constraints. There's a bit of a chicken-and-egg problem here. Because you're not going to want to research fifty ideas, you will need to narrow them down before you dig into numbers. How do you narrow down if you don't know the risks and costs associated with your options?

There are some simple techniques for narrowing your options without needing to immediately engage in all the due diligence for each.

DECISION-MAKER PREFERENCES ON DECISION RECOMMENDATIONS

It's important to consider what your decision-makers want in front of them when you're narrowing options. Many decision-makers want just the "top three." This usually means a solid recommendation and a couple of backups. Some will want to decide to vote only on your top recommendation, and if they don't approve, send you back to the drawing board. Being clear about what they want to see in front of them is going to help you plan for the number of options to prepare and fully vet.

You may have a decision-maker who wants only fully vetted ideas. If that's the case, devote your time to going all the way through the process with each option. To present options that feel "fully baked," you'll need to do a bit more due diligence.

By contrast, some decision-makers aren't going to want or need to see all the back-end work. They might ask you for a gut reaction, or empower you to do the due diligence yourself, but only want to make a decision based on what's right in front of them.

You'll also want to know what their risk tolerance is. It will change what options you present and how you present them. If an organization, or a leader, has a higher risk tolerance, they may be open to some options that those with low-risk tolerance wouldn't even consider.

Have a clear understanding of who is going to be in the room and what their role is. Who is going to be doing the implementation? Is there a project management office whose approval you'll require before moving forward with options? These factors impact the process of narrowing options.

Have a conversation (or several conversations) with your decision-makers, asking before you begin. Use these conversations to get a read on their preferences. Give them clear expectations of how the process of narrowing down options is going to go. Ask them how many options they want to see in front of them, and what level of detail they want to see for each. Come to a clear understanding of how many times you'll interact during the decision-making process and how much input they expect to have during the process.

SANITY CHECK AGAINST CRITERIA

Performing a "sanity check" is a great way to stress-test your options, by comparing each to your original intent and your success criteria. In Step One, you clearly defined what success looks like based on your success criteria. In the sanity check, you'll take each of your options and see how they hold up in the face of those criteria.

If you implemented this option today, will it help you meet the original intent of this decision? Is it going to help you move toward the success metrics you decided on? This is a more subjective process than voting, but you'll be able to eliminate several options just by looking at them through this lens.

VOTING TO NARROW THE OPTIONS

Voting is a powerful tool to narrow options. It allows you to see what a majority of the decision-makers (or the "input" working group, if your decision-makers have decided to delegate this step of the process) are leaning toward. Voting leads to clarity. People want decision-making to be linear. Usually, it's not. When you vote on options there is a clear goal, and that can be comforting in the midst of a sometimes murky process.

There are a lot of ways to vote. For high-impact decisions, you'll want to find a method that is clear, visible, and indisputable.

Let's say you have fifty options up on a wall and ten people in the room. You want to narrow those fifty options down to five before you start doing any kind of research or putting them into a matrix. Give each participant several voting "dots." (When we say "dots" we really do mean those little round-colored stickers. The kind you used in grade school.)

You can hand out as many or as few dots as you want—just be clear that each dot is a vote. Have them walk up to the wall and use their stickers to vote. If you hand out five dots per person, they're allowed to put one dot on each of their five top options. Or, maybe allow them to put all dots on one option if they feel strongly about it. Just make sure the rules are clear before the voting begins!

Decide beforehand how many options you're striving to end up with before you vote. This will most likely be aligned to the decision-maker(s) preferences. Make it clear to everyone in the room what your purpose is.

Once everyone has placed their stickers, you'll count, as a group, and begin to narrow down. Start with the option with the most stickers. That is your number one option. Continue from there until you have your top five (or whatever the agreed-upon number is, that you are narrowing down to).

Those top options go in your decision-making matrix. Look to see if there are any deal breakers based on constraints. If there are, pull those options out and research any remaining. From there, you may begin detailed research and planning.

Tip: You can alternately use a scoring mechanism to average individual scores for each option. In that scenario, you might give people a certain number of points with which to vote, instead of stickers. Decision-makers assign a percentage of their points to their top options. If each person has one hundred points, they can give 25 percent of their points to an option, or 50 percent, etc., until they've assigned all one hundred. Once everyone has assigned their points, just like with the dots, you'll add up the points assigned to each option, and designate your highest-scored option as your winner.

SOCIALIZING OPTIONS WITH STAKEHOLDERS

Expose stakeholders to the options, before and after they are narrowed down. Ask questions. *"What's the worst that could happen if we implement this?"* Getting input from people who are going to be affected by the decision but are not themselves the decision-makers is a great way to involve others when identifying potential risks.

Allow your stakeholders to voice their thoughts. Don't only focus on the agreed-upon options. If you've gone through a voting process, take the time to ask questions about the options that didn't get any votes. "Why wouldn't this option succeed?" Get additional thoughts in the room. You're looking to *disqualify* options, as much as to qualify. It is also helpful to understand a stakeholder's thought process.

HIGH-EMOTION MOMENTS

Remember: narrowing isn't easy. For many people, this is the most challenging part of the process. Don't let that scare you! Yes, emotions are going to run high. If you are aware of that ahead of time, you can come prepared to soothe any hot feelings by grounding the group. Keep going back to the intent of the decision, and the most important criteria.

As you narrow down your options, people may get distracted by bigger and shinier toys. They will head down unnecessary rabbit holes. They will start talking through a tangential idea that's unrelated to what you're trying to accomplish simply because they feel a strong emotion about it. That's your cue to ground. Keep coming back to that objective criteria. Remind the group why you're all here.

If you've established your must-have criteria ahead of time, you are less likely to go astray. You can continue to bring people back to it. Use it to help you qualify and disqualify particular options.

Feel free to get creative. Combine your options. Find new ways to vote. Keep one eye on separating emotions from the actual predetermined criteria. Then stress-test your options. *Does this meet the original intent of the decision?*

Some people are going to feel that you're moving too slowly. Some people are going to think it's all moving too fast, and some will have a strong emotional connection to a particular option. To get to a good decision, you have to recognize and then get some distance from the emotional reactions in the room. Use your must-haves to counteract flaring emotions. Remember, criteria aren't emotional, they are objective.

At the end of all of this, if you've done your job correctly, you're going to end up with a short list of really good options.

STEP RECAP...

Before we move on, let's recap the most important elements and action items in this step.

STEP FOUR: NARROWING YOUR LIST

In this step, you'll go from all of the possible options to a small list of the best choices. You'll need to prioritize the list you've made. Come back to your criteria and your intent to show you what is most important.

You can safely eliminate any option that does not have one of your "must-haves" or does have one of your "won't-haves." Then, you will figure out which options best meet your other criteria and needs. This is where your decision matrix will come in handy if you use one. (We recommend using one with a complex decision, as it can be numerically focused.)

Finally, before you move on to the next step, do one last pass to eliminate options. See if any can be combined into one, better option. Then stack-rank what is left.

WHAT'S NEXT?

In the next chapter, we'll discuss getting buy-in from stakeholders. In this section, you'll be learning how to socialize your ideas to gain approval from a larger group. We'll talk about what to do when you're facing resistance, and we'll walk you through how to identify additional risks. Lastly, we'll teach you how to do your homework so that you're prepared, when you move to this next step of the process, to get confident buy-in from all the necessary stakeholders.

Read on to find out how.

CHAPTER EIGHT

STEP FIVE

GAIN BUY-IN

THE NUMBER ONE CHALLENGE WE HEAR FROM LEADERS, across industries, is that getting consensus sometimes feels impossible. We all know that consensus is the ideal state when making decisions, but in reality, it's rarely attainable. In most cases, there will be disagreement, often right up to the moment of decision.

In 2005, Learnit was teaching primarily hands-on software classes: Excel, PowerPoint, and Adobe. In every class, students would get a hardcopy manual relating to the course content. The manuals were printed onsite and a stock was maintained, to ensure there were plenty for upcoming trainings. They also shipped the manuals to other locations where trainings were held. The books were large and bulky. They took up room on desks. Students had to navigate from learning Excel on their monitors to flipping pages in a book. The printing was expensive, the shipping was bad for the environment, and every time a feature changed in Excel (or any other software), the outdated books would be thrown away.

To Damon, this was starting to seem like an antiquated way of doing business. He remembers how often at the end of a class, manuals would just be littered around, left on desks. To the students, they were disposable. There had to be a better way.

To reduce workload internally, Damon and the Operations Team at Learnit found a vendor to support the maintenance of soft copies of the manuals. They also determined it would be great for students to have digital manuals on one computer monitor and the software they were learning on a second monitor during training sessions. This would mean bigger upfront costs for additional monitors for their students, but the other costs that went with the physical manuals—labor, shipping, stocking—would disappear. Not to mention the reduced toll on the environment. It was a perfect solution. Finally, they announced to their instructors: *three months from now, all Learnit classes will eliminate printed manuals and go digital. We hope you're excited!*

They were not.

There was near mutiny. The instructors were adamant: *this is not how we do it.* They were used to their books. Their students were used to their books. They needed their books. This may be in the best interest of Learnit, they told Damon, but it is not in the best interest of the students. Several instructors announced their intention to leave the company if they were forced to use "digital copies" of materials.

Damon was confused and a little angry. How could the instructors not see that this decision was best for everyone? Sure it was a change, but there were a lot of benefits. The digital books would save Learnit money and paper, and allow for updates to materials in real-time. Not only that, but those materials would never get lost or damaged, and they would be searchable. No more flipping page after page to find an answer to a simple question. Control-F was all you needed! Besides, they had already purchased the additional monitors. Learnit had spent tens of thousands of dollars to do so, which was a huge investment for such a small company. It was a big swing, and the pushback from the instructors was not something Damon had planned for.

That was his big mistake.

He and his team had gone ahead with what amounted to a huge change for Learnit and hadn't consulted with the stakeholders who were most directly affected: the instructors. Now, some of the very best teachers working for Learnit—popular with students, well-trained, and effective—were threatening to find other jobs. Damon didn't want that. He also didn't want to be stuck using physical books for the next ten or fifteen years. He knew it was time to modernize.

After the fairly disastrous meeting with the teachers, Damon had to take a step back. He took a breath and considered his options. There was a lead instructor by the name of Jim Olay, who had been with Learnit for several years and was well respected by the group. An influencer. Damon pulled him aside. If he could get Jim in his corner maybe, just maybe, the other instructors would follow. He wasn't just interested in making Jim a convert. Damon truly wanted to know, *what was he missing?* He asked Jim if he could buy him dinner and discuss the issue.

After a drink and some small talk, Damon jumped in. He told Jim that he trusted him and knew he had a really good gauge of what was best for the students. *Where did I go wrong?* He wanted Jim to tell him—without any fear of Damon taking it personally—how they had gone astray. How could Damon feel so clear about this great idea, when the people who mattered most were so adamantly against it?

Jim did share his concerns, but, as their conversation went on—because Damon had already done the heavy lifting to make him feel heard—Jim started pitching a few of the benefits of the new digital manual *to Damon*. He acknowledged that searching would be easier, desks less cluttered, and that the overall experience for the students *might* be better with the digital manuals.

Jim pitched a new tactic to Damon. "I can see the benefits to Learnit," he said. "There's obviously a gigantic cost saving there, but if we lead with the benefits to the instructors—not having to lug around the content, not having to show up at classes where the manuals didn't arrive—instead of focusing on the cost-benefit to Learnit, maybe we could convince them how *they* benefit?"

Damon was relieved to have an ally.

The next day, Jim was the one to address the instructors. He talked through the new idea, from their perspective, focusing on benefits for them and their classrooms. Because he did, they were able to get buy-in from this very important group of stakeholders. Although Jim didn't have any authority over the instructors, he was serving as an influencer. Learnit was one of the first companies in the space to go completely digital around course content. They became an industry leader.

Whether you're a thirty-person company or a 30,000-person company, your stakeholders want to feel heard. You need to put yourself in the shoes of the people who are affected by your decisions. It doesn't matter how confident you are, initiatives fail if there isn't buy-in and support from everyone involved.

If Damon had pressed on, without buy-in, he would have lost valuable employees, diminished morale, and tarnished

Learnit's reputation. *People* are essential to making companies work.

THE DANGER OF SILOED DECISION-MAKING

Leaders are often tempted to sit in their offices and make decisions that sound good to the person whose opinion they value most: their own. This is an extreme example of siloed decision-making. There is no external input, no stakeholders, and no other perspectives to consider.

We know you're not one of those kinds of leaders.

In reality, siloed decisions aren't usually so nefarious. With the best of intentions, decision-makers often make the mistake of seeking opinions from only one group of stakeholders. If a company is rolling out a new software product, for example, there are many stakeholders involved: customers, sales teams, marketing departments, and experts in research and development (R&D). If they focus only on meeting and understanding pain points within the operations team, that's a kind of siloed decision-making. It's dangerous because you're leaving out valuable perspectives. The operations team, consciously or not, is going to be biased toward options that best serve their needs but may not be ideal for other stakeholders.

THE BASICS OF BUY-IN

Understanding how all the stakeholders will be impacted, how a solution is going to benefit them, and what constraints they may be operating under, is your number one job during the buy-in process. You need to know what your stakeholders want and need. This doesn't mean that just because they have an item on their wish list, you must fulfill it. It just means you'll add it to the list (even if it is determined to be out of scope and added to the "won't-have" section). You'll be transparent about what you can and can't guarantee, and you'll enter into all conversations with an open mind.

Your goal should be transparent and an ongoing communication between you and all stakeholders. If you're making decisions in a silo, you're only taking in one, potentially skewed point of view. When in reality, your best path to success is collecting varied input, from as many legitimate sources as you have access to.

Varied input is of benefit to decision-makers, but also to the stakeholders themselves. Seeking buy-in builds trust. It lets people know that their opinion is as valuable as your own—or that of the decision-maker—and when you make people feel valued, you build trust.

BUILDING TRUST

If you want to be a part of an organization that values building trust, this kind of buy-in from stakeholders should be part of your company culture. People in your organization should understand that buy-in is necessary for success. To establish that kind of trust, start by being totally transparent. Let everyone know that when a big decision is being made, their ideas and input will be sought out and considered. You can talk about it, and debate it, but let them know that at the end of the day when you make this decision as an organization, they will need to get behind it. Socialize your options early and often. Let people know what you're trying to accomplish and why you need their support. This is the way the most successful companies can innovate, with the full support of their teams.

LEAD WITH THE WHY

Of course, not all change is good change. Sometimes being transparent means not sugarcoating realities. *We have to lay people off and if we don't, we're going out of business.* In these cases, you have to give people the truth. Tell them what happens if you don't take action. There will always be decisions that aren't popular and aren't going to benefit everyone in your organization. In those cases, it's even more important to lead with the "why." *Note:* We understand that not all decisions can be widely socialized in advance, nor should they. Layoffs are a good example of one of these decisions. But transparency and authenticity are key when these decisions are announced.

Without a storyline, people's imaginations go wild. They gossip. They descend into negativity. They resist. Getting the truth out and consistently sharing it is the best antidote. This means that everyone is sharing the message. The leadership team, project teams, and decision-makers—all need to be sharing the same storyline and the why behind it.

Create talking points and share them with the team. Share them with the people who will be engaged in the most conversations on the subject, and make sure the explanation of the "why" is clear and consistent. If people are expected to come up with their own explanation for the reasons behind a decision, those stories are going to vary dramatically. Being truthful, especially about a difficult upcoming decision, adds to the feeling of transparency among your teams. It builds trust. People are going to feel confident that you have answers, and aren't out there hiding critical information.

This kind of transparency also allows you to identify any risks up ahead. If you're communicating ideas before locking in a decision, stakeholders feel free to wave the red flag. They might bring up concerns you hadn't yet considered. Early feedback allows you to course correct and refine your solutions before it's too late.

WHO TO TALK TO

From a sales perspective, not being able to reach influencers within a (client) company can be the reason a deal falls apart. The stakeholders within that company need to have buy-in, and it's the influencers who are going to reach them. At some point in the sales process, you need to stop and ask who else is going to be impacted and if conversations have been had with them. If they haven't, offer to reach out. Tell them you'll address any concerns, directly. Your goal is to reach the influencers and get them on your team.

If you're already part of the culture, you'll know who has influence in your organization based on the level of respect they engender in the people around them.

Though keep in mind, influencers aren't always those with the most authority. Influencers within an organization are generally the people who are respected and others listen to. While a person with authority might be able to say, *you're going to do this because I'm your boss,* an influential person will be able to deftly influence the other person in your direction. They'll get them to *want* to do what you want them to do. They'll get them excited about the benefits of your solution, and help them understand all the reasons behind it. When you're looking for people with influence, what you're really looking for are *the people that other people listen to.*

WHAT'S IN IT FOR ME?

Wait: before you start reaching across tables and winning over influencers, you have to take a moment and put yourself in their shoes. You need to exercise your empathy. Remember that what people care about most is their experience. They want to know the answer to WIIFM, "What's In It For Me?"

How are they going to be impacted? How are they going to benefit? Is it going to be a giant inconvenience? If you're approaching leaders, they are going to care about all of these questions regarding themselves and their teams.

Learnit has helped many companies roll out new technology. Often they're spending millions of dollars to do it and the benefit is clear, but in almost every case, one of the top concerns is: how inconvenient is this going to be? Because the experience of the people in their company matters to them. They know that people's first thought is going to be: *I have to learn this whole new software?* (You can insert an "ugh" in there wherever it feels appropriate.)

Almost always, the biggest question on everyone's mind is: *What's in it for me?*

HOW TO START

The success of your initiative depends on getting people on board with your idea. How do you go about doing it? From our many years of combined experience, we've come up with a few tried and tested methods for improving your success at getting buy-in. These aren't sure bets, but if you start from a place of connection, empathy, and trust, your odds are going to be a heck of a lot better.

FACE-TO-FACE IS BEST

Have face-to-face conversations if at all possible. This can mean in the same room, or on a video call—the virtual version of "face-to-face." When trying to get someone on board with a big change or a high-impact decision, take fifteen minutes and have this kind of one-on-one meeting. If face-to-face isn't possible, jump on the phone. One fifteen-minute conversation will do so much more for you than a flurry of email exchanges. First, you'll build trust by the sheer act of setting the meeting. You're letting them know right out of the gate that this is important and their opinion matters. In-person or on video, you can read their cues and pick up on enthusiasm (or discomfort) in a way you never could over email.

Take them out for coffee. Grab a virtual drink. The personal rapport you'll develop, even in fifteen minutes, will benefit everyone. People want to know who they'll be working with, especially if you're going to be making a high-impact decision together or implementing big change. People want to know and trust who they're partnering with, so take the time to listen and understand what's driving them.

HOW TO TALK TO THEM

Knowing your own tendencies when it comes to communication can give you key insights into how to talk to your influencers. Just like personalities, communication styles vary from person to person. There are three well-known styles: passive, assertive, and aggressive.

Passive: You Win, I Lose

When you communicate passively, you may have weak boundaries and vague communication. People with this communication style often accommodate others, even when it inconveniences them, and may end up becoming resentful.

Aggressive: I Win, You Lose

People with an aggressive communication style have overly rigid boundaries. They compete to get their way, walking right up to the line of out-and-out disrespect for others. Their manner can be forceful and uncompromising.

Aggressive communicators may seem reasonable on the surface. They might not yell or throw punches, but only the person on the receiving end gets to decide how aggressive is too aggressive. The good news is that there are ways to be direct, without being perceived as aggressive.

Assertive: We Both Win

Assertive people are respectful to both others and themselves. They look for "win-win" situations. They set and respect appropriate boundaries. This is the style you should be aiming for, and it can be learned.

With assertiveness, there is no gray area. There are no misunderstandings because the message is clear. You're voicing your actual needs while also listening to others. Assertive people operate from a stable, healthy place and tend to attract the same.

In decision-making, collaboration is key to getting the best results. Brainstorming, looking for root causes, prioritizing, and narrowing down options all greatly benefit from solid assertive communication. Spending the time to develop boundary-setting skills and respectful communication will more than pay off in the quality of decisions.

AGGRESSIVENESS STYLE AND PERSONALITY

Remember how we said aggression is in the eye of the beholder? The D type of DiSC personality tends to be very direct in how they communicate with others. Sometimes, that can come off as aggressive to other types, even when they do not intend to disrespect others. To be heard effectively, D types may need to soften their style depending on their audience.

In contrast, S types tend to be more accommodating than other styles. They prefer to be peacekeepers and may be reserved in their opinions. It's common for S types to struggle to set firm boundaries. So, given their natural tendencies, S types will need to practice being assertive. They must set and defend boundaries, deliver clear messages, and respect themselves and others mindfully.

Each personality type has its own strengths and potential blind spots, which is why self-awareness is so important. Each must adjust their style to some degree to allow their voice to be heard. Each must work to develop assertiveness skills for the best outcomes, whether those feel natural to their type or not.

ASSERTIVENESS SKILL: ACTIVE LISTENING

One of the most important skills in assertive communication is active listening. Active listening means listening to *understand the situation* rather than listening just to respond. In active listening, you're not waiting for a pause in the conversation so you can jump in—you're taking in what the other person has to say. Active listening also means asking thoughtful questions and being engaged in the conversation.

Make no mistake though, assertiveness isn't about just listening and agreeing. Nodding your head and keeping your mouth shut to seem like you're actively listening is a cop-out. It's probably also pretty transparent to the other person. An assertive interaction goes two ways and underscores mutual respect.

ASSERTIVENESS SKILL: BOUNDARIES

Boundaries are a particularly important (and tricky) skill to master. Much of the boundary guidance that has been written addresses personal relationships. Both are vital areas to master boundary-setting, yet everyday workplace relationships also require healthy boundaries to succeed.

For example, let's say you already have fifty hours of work on your plate this week. If one of your colleagues approaches you and asks you to take twenty hours of their work because their eight-year-old daughter is sick, how you handle the situation is a great example of boundaries in action.

A passive person might feel they need to take on the extra work, powering through a seventy-hour workweek, sacrificing time with their friends and family, or their hobbies. Their weak boundaries mean that not only do they not say no, but they also won't try to rearrange the workload or manage expectations with anyone. They will work themselves to the bone to try to make it work at their own cost. An aggressive person will not only refuse but berate the other person for asking in the first place. An aggressive person might also try to use their boundaries to control the other person's behavior, for example, to try to get the person to stay at work instead of caring for their daughter. Or, they might use passive-aggressive communication to try to make the other person feel bad about asking. None of this is productive, and it can lead to a toxic work environment if repeated often enough.

If you are assertive, on the other hand, you might offer to help in a healthier way. "I completely understand the situation. Let's come up with a clear plan by deciding what is in the "must complete" status this week and what we may be able to push deadlines on to ensure nobody gets burned out. I have some ideas. Are you free now to collaborate, or would tomorrow morning be better, once your daughter is settled? Once aligned, we can propose the solution to our manager."

Boundaries do become tricky in practice, and many people handle them differently, so it's worth thinking about your own style of boundary-setting. We recommend the book *Conflict Resolution Playbook: Practical Communication Skills* by Stanford's Jeremy Pollack for a more in-depth treatment of boundaries and conflict resolution in the workplace. Pollack gives many specific language recommendations that we have found helpful. There are also many other useful resources on the topic available elsewhere.

BODY LANGUAGE

The other benefit of an in-person or video meeting is that you have access to the superpower of body language. No need to be an expert in the subject! It's simple: if you're having a conversation with someone and their legs and arms are crossed—or they're sitting in that chair looking ready to pounce—that speaks volumes. Go in with preventative ease. Embody a more relaxed state. Be open, in your mind and body. Most likely, if you're having a conversation with someone, especially around change, they are going to reflect the body language that they see in you.

On the flip side, if someone is telling you, *yeah that sounds great*, but they're slumped in their chair or clearly ill at ease—you may need to dig a little deeper. They may not be giving you the whole story.

This kind of "people reading" is more challenging but not impossible. When you're in a video meeting, you can still be aware and alert both to what people are saying out loud and what their body language is telling you.

There was a study done in 1968 by Dr. Albert Mehrabian, who was a specialist in nonverbal communication, which showed that only 7 percent of communication is from words. *Seven percent.* The study showed 38 percent comes from tone of voice, and 55 percent comes from body language. This means that if you're not able to see and hear the person you're trying to convince, you're losing 93 percent of their communication. Take the time to look and to listen. Long story short: you're never going to know if you have a person's authentic buy-in from words alone.

This applies to you, too. Make eye contact. If the person you're talking to is standing, you stand. If they're sitting, you sit. Be on their level and give them 100 percent of your attention. Don't quickly finish up an email while they're standing there in your office, nodding your head and pretending to listen. Utilize that extra 55 percent of communication by leading with your body language, and be available. Also, be mindful of your tone of voice. Are you coming across as frustrated? Excited? Exhausted? People notice this.

AUTHENTICITY

Be authentic. We can't stress this enough. Human beings are smart and are hardwired to pick up on inauthenticity. It's a survival instinct, with evolutionary roots going back to predators and prey. In today's world, people can spot inauthenticity a mile away. Don't try and make a bad situation seem like a good one. Don't tell people what you think they want to hear. Your goal is to build trust, and trust requires honesty and transparency. Lead with benefits, but if there's a downside—give it to them straight.

TIMING

Pick your timing carefully when it comes to a buy-in conversation. People know this instinctively when it comes to their personal lives. If you want to go to an Aerosmith concert (because come on, they've still got it), you're not going to broach that question with your significant other at 5:30 p.m. when you've both just gotten home from work, haven't had time to decompress, and are exhausted. You know better. That's not a moment when you're going to have a receptive audience. However, if you've both just had a nice dinner, maybe there's been a glass of wine and some jokes exchanged...the conversation is going to go a heck of a lot better.

That's timing. (If you want to read a really good book on the subject, try *Pre-Suasion: A Revolutionary Way to Influence and Persuade*, by Robert Cialdini, PhD.)

The same is true in a professional setting. No matter how good your idea is, you are not going to find buy-in if you approach someone right after they've come off of a negative interaction. If they've had a tough day or a tough week, it's not the time to schedule a meeting at 4:45 p.m. and throw out a: *hey, what do you think about this big decision we have in front of us?*

To illustrate, say you're the CEO of a small business. You've just come off a poor month and the economy looks terrible. *Still.* Is this a good time for the marketing team to come to you and ask about a big investment in new software? Absolutely, definitely, not. Now, if your marketing lead was smart and decided to wait two weeks until after you close that big deal that's been in the works...the answer might be different.

This is something we've seen time and time again. Whether working with your own internal teams or an external company—you can get two very different answers regarding big decisions, solely based on timing.

DECISION-MAKING ROLES

As previously discussed, there are multiple roles in the decision-making process: the *decision-maker*, people who are providing *input*, people who are *driving* the decision and recommendations forward, and the *implementer*. When you're trying to generate buy-in, you need transparency around your role and the role of the person you're speaking to.

Be specific: I'm not the decision-maker on this. However, I'm going to be pulling together the top three recommendations and putting them in front of Damon so that he can make the best decision possible by the end of the month.

If you're not the decision-maker, let them know that you'd like their input. Tell them you can't make any promises, but you want to avoid any future misunderstandings by hearing them out.

If you are the decision-maker, start the conversation by saying so. Again, don't make any promises but do let them know what portion of the process they might have control over. Ask them to tell you what you should be thinking about and including as you go forward.

Regardless of your position, if you're entering into a buy-in conversation, you are setting the rules of the road. In the process, you are establishing boundaries: *this is what you do, this is what I do.* It's a great way to avoid confusion or upset later on.

ASKING FOR FEEDBACK

Once you've chosen your meeting place, picked your timing, and established roles, your next job is to listen. You're not entering into these conversations to just present your good ideas and convince them. You should be actively seeking feedback. *Why?* You want the other person to feel heard, which we've covered (and will cover again, it's that important) but you also need them to tell you where your blind spots are. You need their feedback as much, if not more than you need their buy-in.

Use open-ended (yet specific) questions and phrase them so that the other person has the opportunity to think and respond honestly. "Yes or No" queries aren't going to serve you. Engage them in their own expertise. *What are the most important features of this system when it comes to doing your job?*

We also recommend the very straightforward: *based on what you know, what could go wrong here?* Get them to talk about the risks you haven't accounted for. As we discussed in Chapter Seven, the earlier you can get a handle on potential obstacles, the easier it will be to make plans to mitigate them. Use these buy-in conversations as another opportunity to get people talking about the iceberg you haven't spotted.

Then once you've covered the specifics, get broad, so that no thought is left unsaid. There are great ways to pull more conversation out of someone with simple open-ended questions. *Is there anything else that we haven't talked about that you think is important for me to know? What else am I missing? Is there anything else on your mind related to this topic?*

Conversations around buy-in should bring to your attention the risks that need to be addressed. You may head into the conversation all set to get people excited and make them feel heard—as you should—but if you've done your job well, the person on the other side should feel safe enough to get real with you. That's when you'll get their honest feedback. That's when you'll hear what the risks and alternatives are.

AVOIDING CONFIRMATION BIAS

One word of caution: as you enter into the buy-in phase, especially for high-impact decisions, be on the lookout for your own bias. If there are three people on a team your decision will impact, and you know that one of them tends to be a "yes" person, avoid the temptation to have the buy-in conversation only with them. Seek out the people who will give you honest feedback. You're not just looking for the yes. You need pushback, if it's out there, so that you can adjust and plan for a reapproach as necessary.

When Kandis is working with a newer client and trying to get a good understanding of the current state before diving into a process improvement project, she likes to ask the project sponsor for a list of people to whom she can speak to. More specifically, she asks for confirmation that there will be a few names on the list of people who give feedback often and may be considered somewhat difficult to work with. She appreciates honest feedback and you should too!

ALWAYS MOVE FORWARD

The hope is always that the buy-in conversations are going to be just one step in a linear process. You get the buy-in, confirm the solidity of your options, and move forward to make your decision. This isn't always the case. Sometimes the benefit of these conversations (and it is a benefit) is that you learn new information that needs to be considered before moving forward. Sometimes the confirmation is that this is not a smart way to proceed, and in those cases, it's back to the drawing board. Don't despair! You're not moving backward in time, you're returning to the information-gathering phase (Step Two), armed with even more knowledge than you had the first time.

In that scenario, you'll return to what you learned in the previous chapters. Gather information, create a new list of possible options, narrow them down, and go back to get buy-in on your new idea.

STEP RECAP...

Before we move on, let's recap the most important elements and action items in this step.

STEP FIVE: GETTING BUY-IN

Buy-in is critical to making sure a project or decision will ultimately succeed. If you move forward on a decision and the team is not enthusiastic about it, they may not put forth the effort needed for implementation. If they're not clear about what was decided, they may act in the wrong direction. (Kandis and Damon have both seen good decisions fail for no other reason than that they lacked buy-in or understanding of the decision.)

If you want people to be behind any major decision, and

to give their best effort, take the time to do this step correctly. You can't be a keyboard warrior. You'll need to talk to people and make connections one on one. Be transparent about what you want to accomplish. Directly ask them for their support.

Being senior in your position does not exempt you from this need. You may be the boss, and you may think that others will just fall in line, but unfortunately, that's not how it works. Have the conversations. Hear people out. Talk them through what you intend, and get them excited. Uncover who your naysayers are and address the issue with them directly. (If you can change their minds, you can turn your biggest implementation risk into an asset.)

WHAT'S NEXT?

Learnit was able to shake itself free from analog teaching methods, and those clunky textbooks, by focusing less on its great idea, and more on its great people. That is, after all, what buy-in is all about. No idea thrives on an island. Or in a silo. You need your team of supporters if you are going to take the long walk toward that successful end state. It only took one face-to-face meeting between Damon and Jim for the tide to turn in his direction. Damon made a valuable influencer in his company feel heard, with no strings attached, and in the process, he gained an ally, and a clear way forward.

Trust that your allies are out there. Approach them with an open mind, and listen to what they have to say. They just might guide you exactly where you want to go.

In the next chapter, we'll get to the meat of the matter: making the decision. Read on to find out all the nitty-gritty details about the big moment and how best to prepare yourself.

CHAPTER NINE

STEP SIX

MAKE THE DECISION

GROWING UP, DAMON WAS AN AVID BASEBALL CARD COL-
lector. It was something he did with his dad. A bonding activity
and a shared interest. As the years went on, he developed quite
a significant collection. Every year, his dad would buy him the
card set from that season. Together, they'd go to baseball card
conventions (this was the eighties) in Los Angeles, and buy
up the hard-to-get cards. Damon can still remember sitting
with his dad at the hotel—flowered bedspread and all—carefully
putting each card into its plastic sleeve. It was special. Just for
the two of them.

It was a kid activity though, and people grow up. In 2011,
Damon was nearing forty and the collection was taking up
much-needed space in his tiny San Francisco condo. It was
doing little more than collecting dust, still pristine in all
those binders. He went online and found someone willing to
purchase the entire collection for $30,000. *Thirty-thousand
dollars.* He didn't need those cards anymore, did he? His father

had recently passed. Who knew if he would have a son or a daughter or a grandchild to pass them on to. Damon sold the collection. After all, they were losing value. They were just... taking up space.

Cut to now. Eleven years later. If Damon still had his card collection, it could easily be worth over $150,000. For Damon, though, the regret of selling his collection isn't financial. He does have a son now, one whom he'd love to hand them down to. It wouldn't have been just a collection of cards...it would have been a legacy. Passed from father to son, and son again. His father has been gone for many years, and maybe having that collection would be a way to stay connected. It would be a tactile reminder of all those weekends spent in hotels, slipping card after card into plastic. Just recently, while having lunch with a close friend and his son (Damon's godson), the friend told a story of passing down his own, much smaller, card collection to his son. It opened a pit in Damon's stomach.

Selling those cards was a bad decision.

Damon might argue there is just as much risk in making a decision too soon. For his part, he sold the baseball card collection well before gathering 70 percent of the information he should have had (as outlined in Step Two). Had he followed the advice we lay out here in earlier chapters, and thought through some other options for storing the cards, he may have found an alternative. He could have reconfigured how they were housed or found a willing friend with a dry basement or attic. Also, had he taken a moment to consider future risks—like not having the collection to pass down to his own son, or the loss of the connection to his own father through the cards—he might have made a different choice.

PULL THE LEVER

We've talked a lot in this book about *process*, and all the steps leading up to making a decision. We are now at the point where you put your money where your mouth is and *make* the decision. It is time to take action.

The truth is, you could gather all of the best information and take all the absolute right steps, but if you're not clear on how the decision is going to be made...the process is going to get messy. You have to be able to pull the lever that says GO. If you're not able to—if you hesitate or rush at the last minute— you can lose some of the buy-ins you've worked so hard to gain. You risk leaving a bad taste in people's mouths. That's why, when it comes down to it, you have to be organized and able to get across that finish line...without leaving regret in your wake.

NO MORE SURPRISES

By this point, you should have a good idea of who's involved in the decision-making process. You should know who the influencers are in your organization. You should have gathered all of your information and taken the temperature of the key stakeholders. You should know what direction they're leaning and what they think a successful outcome looks like. There shouldn't be any surprises.

What, then, does making the decision look like?

Oftentimes, group decisions are made in a meeting, so being organized and planning a specific decision-making meeting is important. To prepare, you'll want to think through who needs to be in the room. You'll also want to create an agenda in advance and be crystal clear on the desired outcome of the meeting itself. Is this just to talk about the decision and make the decision later? Or is this the moment you are going to make the decision? That distinction needs to be made clear to attendees. They are going to want to think through their positions before the meeting.

You're also going to want to lay down some ground rules about how the decision is going to be made once in the meeting. There are many factors to consider. Are you trying to reach a consensus? If so, great if you can make that happen. However, consensus is often challenging if not impossible to reach (as previously covered). Have a backup plan. If consensus isn't possible, can you lean into voting?

To give yourself the best chance at success, you may want to block out some time on your calendar just to think through all the moving parts. Doing this earlier in the day, while you're not experiencing decision fatigue, is ideal. During this "meeting with yourself," you'll also want to review the recommendations you've gotten from stakeholders. If you are both driver and decision-maker, you'll want to take this time to review the information you've gathered so that you can feel comfortable, confident, and able to explain the "why" behind the direction you've chosen. This review session should last, depending on the decision, between ninety minutes and two hours.

DECISION-MAKING ROLES

We determined earlier in this process that when you're getting buy-in, you should be specifically targeting the decision-makers and understanding what type of information they need in front of them to make the best decision. When you're at the decision-making stage, you want to have a very clear idea of all the roles in the room. The driver of the decision will most likely be presenting all the options to the decision-makers. However, sometimes people will be playing dual roles. The driver of the decision may also be one of the decision-makers. In this case, a facilitator can help get people across the finish line so that there is no appearance of bias. The person in this consultant role should also be one of the people in the room when you are pulling your options together. They should be the ones helping move choices through legal or HR so that you can have full confidence all the options have been appropriately "blessed" before moving toward a vote.

As a reminder, the decision-making roles typically break down into:

- Decision-maker (Who may also be the driver of the decision.)
- Input
- Driver
- Implementers

DECISION FACILITATORS

An objective outside facilitator can be brought in to help with your decision-making meeting. This is a person who isn't going to be voting. They are simply there to help. Kandis has gone in as a facilitator to support people organizations in their decision-making meetings. If you have access to someone like her, who is an expert in decision-making, or even an HR business partner who would be willing to help—an unbiased supporter can be key in these situations. They can be there to support the process and help everyone understand exactly how the decision is going to be made. Most importantly, after the decision is made, they can help reiterate the direction you will be moving in.

Think of this person as a mediator: a professional in their field, without a stake in your decision. In the same way, a judge is there to keep a courtroom in order while leaving the actual decision-making up to the jury. A facilitator can be a set of watchful eyes and someone to implement order and structure in a process that can sometimes feel chaotic.

This person should go around the room and make sure everyone is on board. They should get a yes from everyone. When Kandis does this, she goes around the room: *yes, yes, yes, yes, yes, yes.* They should then review what talking points should be consistently used when they leave the room. They should know how the decision is going to be announced for the first time and should align on what each person will say when someone asks them about it. Usually, the facilitator will work with the leader in the room to come up with three to five talking points that can be used. You don't want anyone out there making up their own story, off the cuff.

This kind of outside help can be very reassuring to the leaders because they can rest easy knowing that everyone is going to stay on board and get the appropriate message out. That said, if you've gone around the room and everyone has given their verbal yes for being on board it's ultimately up to the leaders to hold them accountable if they aren't living up to their end of the agreement. Undermining the decision outside of the meeting room is poisonous. The experience with the facilitator will make this kind of defection much less likely.

TYPES OF MEETINGS RELATED TO DECISION-MAKING

It is key to clearly define what type of meeting is being scheduled to support decision-making and appropriately prepare stakeholders in advance. Five common types of meetings support decision-making: (1) strategic, (2) informational, (3) problem-solving, (4) performance, and (5) making a decision.

Types of Meetings That Support Decision-Making

Strategic   Informational   Problem-Solving   Performance   Making Decision

1. **Strategic meetings:** These meetings are focused on long-term planning and goal setting. They can help decision-makers gain a broader perspective on the organization's direction and identify key priorities and initiatives.

2. **Informational meetings:** These meetings are focused on sharing information with stakeholders, such as updates on project progress, market trends, or other relevant data. By providing a common understanding of key facts and figures, informational meetings can help decision-makers make informed choices and avoid potential blind spots.

3. **Problem-solving:** These meetings are designed to address specific challenges or opportunities facing the organization. They can be structured as formal problem-solving sessions or more open-ended brainstorming sessions, but either way, they provide a forum for stakeholders to share ideas, generate creative solutions, and explore different options for addressing the problem or opportunity, which can be used as input to the decision-making process.

4. **Performance meetings:** These meetings are focused on reviewing progress against key metrics or goals, such as project milestones. By providing a regular check-in on performance, these meetings can help decision-makers identify areas where the organization is excelling and where it may need to adjust its approach.

5. **Decision-making meetings:** These meetings are focused

on making a specific decision. By providing a structured framework for decision-making, these meetings can help ensure that decisions are made in a fair, transparent, and well-informed manner.

The decision-making meeting itself might be quite a bit shorter. If you've already gained buy-in and know how all the relevant parties are leaning, you might have a quick thirty-minute discussion, vote, and you're done. However, if you know there are some resistant stakeholders in the room and it's going to be a sticky discussion, you'll want to plan for more time. This all goes back to what we discussed in Chapter Eight, *knowing your audience.*

At the start of the meeting, it should be clear to everyone in the room why you're there and how the decision is going to be made. All should be in agreement that you will be leaving the room with a decision. You may want to say, flat-out, *we're trying to reach a consensus on this.* Explain that the three options have been thoughtfully explored, and recap how you got to this point.

As you're preparing to move toward consensus or a vote, take the time to explain each option. There are three things that people generally need to feel comfortable making a decision:

- Number one is *logic.* Some people will really want you to walk them through the process, step-by-step. *What happened first? How was the problem identified? How did you gather your data?*
- The second is *vision.* For the visionary people in the room, you may need to paint the picture of how different scenarios are going to play out once the decision is made and implemented. *Be detailed; get them excited about the vision.*
- The third is *numbers.* People (almost all of them) are going

to want the numbers: costs, percentages, how many days to implement, etc.

You can use all of these tools to move toward a consensus, but if you know you have some very strong no's in the room (based on the work you did collecting feedback and getting buy-in in Chapter Eight) then you may want to move quickly to voting.

WAYS TO GET TO A DECISION

When it comes to making decisions, there are various approaches that can be employed. Each method has its own advantages and drawbacks, and the choice of approach depends on the context, urgency, and the dynamics of the decision-making process.

CONSENSUS

Getting consensus, or agreement among all stakeholders involved when making a high-impact decision, is a good goal. This ensures that everyone involved has an opportunity to contribute their perspective, ideas, and concerns; it promotes transparency and open communication, which can foster trust and goodwill; and it can lead to better implementation, as everyone is working toward a shared goal.

However, achieving consensus can be quite challenging for several reasons. First, stakeholders often have different priorities, goals, and perspectives, which can make it difficult to find a solution that satisfies everyone. In addition, there may be power dynamics at play, with some individuals or groups having more influence or authority than others, which can create imbalances in the decision-making process. Lastly, there may be time constraints or external pressures that make it difficult to engage in a thorough and collaborative decision-making process.

Although it can be challenging to achieve consensus, it is important for organizations to continue to strive toward this goal. You'll still need to have a backup plan on how the decision will be made if consensus is not possible.

VOTING

Look for either a majority or a plurality. Make it clear in advance which kind of voting you'll be doing. In a majority, more than half of the people in the room must vote one way to choose an option. In a plurality, the largest group of people in the room must vote in one way. For example, say you have three different options and ten people in the room. In this scenario, three people vote on option one, three people vote on option two, and four people vote on option three: option three is the winner. Four people is not a majority (if there were ten people you would need more than five people to vote on the same option to have a majority), but it is the largest group based on how people voted. It's the plurality.

One downside to voting with a plurality is that there may be more people opposed to the direction of the decision than in favor. In the example with ten people voting, only four out of ten people wanted the third option. This can cause challenges. Tips: When voting, consider keeping the group small and at an odd number (that way you won't end up with a tie). You'll also need to be clear on how and when you'll be voting.

Making choices in advance about how voting is going to work ahead of time will avoid the frustration of people feeling like you're changing or making up rules as you go.

Sometimes there is a leader in the room who will set ground rules around voting. They may abstain from voting and decide to follow the majority opinion. They may also set themselves up as the tie-breaker, so if five people vote on option one and five people vote on option two, the leader will be the final vote. Although we recommend voting with odd numbers, we understand this may not always be possible, based on the designated decision-makers.

Weighted Voting

Weighted voting is commonplace in corporate shareholder meetings. In these meetings, each shareholder will vote proportional to the number of shares they own. Shareholders with more shares have more skin in the game, thus their votes count for more.

Weighted voting can also be useful in organizations where the leadership team is going to be voting, but the decision will significantly impact one department or team more than the other. In this case, weighted voting can help shore up parties with more at stake. You may want the COO to have a vote that "weighs" twice as much as anyone else's. They get two times the votes because they are going to be the one who implements the decision and will be impacted the most by its outcomes.

Weighted votes are situational, and the details of how your weighted voting will work should be decided ahead of time.

The decision-making matrix covered in Chapter Seven is an example of a tool that can support weighted voting, either as a group with everyone agreeing on the scoring of each option for each criterion, or individually by each voting stakeholder. If each individual completes the matrix separately, the votes can be consolidated and averaged to determine a clear winner.

Voting Tools

Occasionally, you'll want to make voting more visible. To do this, head to your local office supply store and pick up some colored circle stickers (we also touched on this method, sometimes referred to as dot voting" in Step Four, when prioritizing and narrowing options). At your meeting, hand these out to all voters. You can use this technique for regular voting or weighted voting. If you're implementing weighted voting, you'll just give people with more votes, more stickers. Write your options on a flip chart or a whiteboard and ask voters to put a sticker next to the option they want to move forward with.

This kind of visual vote can help people process how everyone else in the room voted. Even if you aren't moving forward with a particular individual's preferred choice, they can still see that, *okay, all five other people in this room voted for another option*. It can often help people get on board with the decision, whether or not they agree with it.

COMMAND DECISIONS

Most of the time, a leader shouldn't be the only one making the decision. It bleeds buy-in. High-impact decisions are difficult to implement, buy-in allows you to move forward collectively and make sure that implementation is successful. The team will be more likely to be on board with the decision if they have part ownership in making it. Consensus and voting are messy, but the extra time leads to better implementation and better communication. The time is well worth it.

If a big decision is made in a silo, then you only have one person carrying the weight and doing the job of defending their decision. You only have one person gathering information and you will miss out on the benefits that a lack of consensus can bring. Having stakeholders bring up risks and problems is a necessary and useful part of the process.

The two exceptions to this rule are: (1) time-sensitive situations and (2) emergencies. Let's say you have an hour to make a critical decision or you lose your operating budget for the month. (Ouch.) You don't have the time to bring the team in for an extended debate. If you're facing the potential loss of life, you also don't have time to phone three friends. Military-style decision-making occurs in the military for a reason.

When you need an answer *now* or risk crashing into the Hudson, you need one captain on the plane. A crisis is going to demand a quick decision with little or no input. One person can make a decision far faster than a group. The key is to know which situation is which, and not confuse them.

At all costs, you should avoid a slow, no-input decision for high-impact items. Not only is it risky, but you are sure to alienate your allies along the way.

Do not set up false rules or overrule your team after they have made a decision. If you say you'll be the tie-breaking vote, you must follow through. If seven people vote for option one and three people vote for option two, the decision is made. You cannot then say you're going with option two, or make up another option three.

If you do, you destroy all buy-in and frustrate every member of your team. You will lose trust that will take time to get back.

If, for whatever reason, you're going to make the final decision after debate, *you must say so.* Be very clear about the purpose of the meeting. "This is an input-only, brainstorm-only meeting. Once we leave here, I am going to make the decision." Say it in the agenda, and say it again verbally at the beginning. Do not leave any room for confusion.

Lastly, if you find yourself in a situation where you do have to make a command decision, even having one trusted source to bounce ideas off of can be incredibly useful in mitigating some of these risks. Perhaps you're faced with a sensitive decision—you have to lay off hundreds of people—you may not want many other stakeholders to be a part of the process, but you'll want to have a trusted agent on your side. Find someone with whom you can work and think through the decision. You will most likely need to partner with an HR person or another expert in the area. If you're sworn to secrecy at work, talk to your spouse or a trusted friend...someone who isn't going to be impacted at all by the outcome. Find a non-biased person who can double-check your logic and alert you to any glaring blind spots. You don't want a "yes" person, or you may find yourself on the wrong side of a bad decision.

GROUPTHINK

Groupthink is your worst decision-making fear made real.

When people refuse to use their voice and instead get on board with what others are doing, saying, or voting to avoid feeling like an outcast, that is groupthink. It leads to errors in decision-making. It leads to bad decisions. People are particularly susceptible to groupthink when a leader shares their opinion first and makes it clear: *this is what I think we should do... what do you all think?* As a reminder from Chapter Six, one way to avoid groupthink is to silence the leader or invite them to share last. This will prevent everyone from just blindly agreeing with what the leader says.

Make it clear to people, before the meeting, that you want them to use their voices. Let them know that they've been invited to the table *for* their voice. Encourage them to think critically about what's being said. You want them to challenge ideas as they come up. You want them to express whether or not they think an option is going to work. Prime them for that kind of critical thinking.

Another tool you can use to avoid groupthink is to assign someone in the room to play the devil's advocate. Have them push back where pushback is needed. Let them be the ones to talk about where the decision implementation is going to go wrong. Where are the holes in your solution? This empowers people to say what they might not otherwise feel comfortable saying. There is no fear that they are going to be perceived as a naysayer or the negative voice in the room if they are "assigned" this role.

Your facilitator can also set up ahead of time that you're going to have everyone be critical at the front end, to get all the information in the room, but that once you've made the final decision, everyone will need to get on board.

GROUPTHINK VERSUS CONSENSUS

Consensus can be difficult to reach, but a lack of consensus can be more beneficial than a case of groupthink. If you're in a situation where consensus is out of reach because there are people in the room who feel strongly and are standing firmly in their views, you can still vote and come to a decision—even if there are disagreements. With groupthink, no one is even voicing their actual opinion. You'll see this sometimes in a company where there has been a significant scandal and no one inside the organization took any action. Often this is a case of groupthink. *Everyone else is doing it, so who am I to do differently?*

In groupthink situations, people are feeling the need to conform. Whatever the reason. They are not bringing their true voices to the table. When you're getting consensus, you're encouraging people and influencing them to move in a certain direction, however, hopefully, you're still hearing the individual voices of everyone in the room.

Groupthink can be incredibly dangerous for decision-makers. Take the example of Vishal Garg, the CEO of the mortgage lending startup, Better.com. In early 2022, Garg took to a Zoom call and fired 900 employees in an awkward one-way video exchange. He faced major backlash, lost investors, and had to make a public apology to try and salvage his reputation after the blunder. Did he decide to fire 15 percent of his workforce over Zoom in a bubble? Maybe. More than likely, this decision was subject to groupthink. For reasons we can never know, people adjacent to Garg may have held their tongue or silenced their own better instincts when it came time to decide how to inform the affected employees of their imminent termination.

Do your best to eliminate groupthink before it has a chance to take root.

NOT THE END OF THE ROAD

You've worked so hard up to this point to gather information, generate buy-in, and pull together your options. You have to have a plan for getting across the finish line. Be clear about how your decision is going to be made and have a clear plan for successfully executing the decision-making meeting. Know, in specifics, how the decision is going to be made. Will you obtain consensus or is this a command decision? Make the plan visible to everyone who will be affected. Then ensure the decision gets made by presenting the right information so that everyone who is walking out of that room has their marching orders and talking points.

Decisions have a lasting impact. Had Damon taken the time to imagine himself, twelve years down the road, looking into the eyes of his own sports-loving son, he might have made a different decision about those baseball cards. Had he asked a trusted friend, he might have been alerted to the potential future pit in his stomach when he thought back on those trips to baseball card conventions with his dad, without the physical cards to remember him by.

GET ON BOARD, STAY ON BOARD

You are allowed to disagree in the decision-making meeting, but once a decision is made, everyone needs to get on board and be prepared to represent that decision as if it was their own. You may need to say those exact words to the people in the room. Consider it a nonnegotiable rule of the road. You'll need to call people out and hold them accountable if they don't abide by it.

Simply put, get on the bus or get off the bus, because this bus is leaving.

If you have a leader, or anyone for that matter, who leaves the room and starts tearing down the decision that's just been made, it is going to negatively impact everyone involved. It will chip away at successful implementation. No matter their personal feelings, you need everyone who was part of the decision-making process to get on that bus! Disagreements need to be left in the meeting room. You want leaders leaving the room, putting their doubts to the side, and being able to communicate why the decision was made.

Be thorough when talking through each of the options and the reasoning behind them during the meeting to make this post-mortem communication easier for everyone. This is why you'll want to use logic, vision, and numbers to reach everyone in the room. Different people respond to different communication techniques, and you'll want to cover all your bases so that everyone can walk out of that room with a true understanding of the "why" behind the decision.

STEP RECAP...

Before we move on, let's recap the most important elements and action items in this step.

STEP SIX: MAKING THE DECISION

This step is often more intimidating than expected. In many cases, despite your best efforts, you will not feel you have all the information you need. You still have to move forward, or miss opportunities. Take a breath, and make the best decision you can with the information you have. You can always course correct later as you need to. Communication is important at every step of the process, but in this step communication is crucial. Making a decision is a blink in time, and implementation will begin immediately after. Set yourself and your team up for success by communicating the decision thoroughly and immediately.

WHAT'S NEXT?

Remember: make a plan so that you aren't forced to live with avoidable regret. Then take action. Don't wait for the last 30 percent of the information to come trickling in before you make a decision. Trust that you're ready, you've done your homework, and commit.

Congratulations, you've made your decision!

Now it's time to reconnect with your influencers and start implementation. Read on to find out how.

CHAPTER TEN

STEP SEVEN

IMPLEMENT THE DECISION

MOST OF US WERE WILDLY UNPREPARED FOR HOW COVID-19 would impact our personal and professional lives. That's why they called it an "unprecedented" event. The ground shift that happened in the Spring of 2020 was a litmus test of sorts for corporations—how would they cope? Could they cope? Would they fold under the unimaginable weight of global shutdown, or could they pivot and take it in stride? There is no better example of this than at Zoom.

When the global pandemic took hold, people were suddenly working at home who had never worked from home before. It became a mammoth cultural shift, and for whatever reason, we all chose Zoom as our preferred video communication method.

Zoom grew from a maximum of ten million daily meeting participants in December 2019 to more than 200 million per day in March 2020. Zoom didn't stop there. In fiscal year 2022, they delivered strong results with total revenue of more than $4 billion growing 55 percent year over year along with increased profitability and operating cash flow growth.

To handle this much growth, they had to take on significant numbers of new employees and open offices all over the country.[25]

Lesser companies might have collapsed with such rocket-speed acceleration. Zoom didn't. Why not? Because they were making good decisions quickly and implementing them well. They had their challenges of course—security concerns, zoom bombers in classrooms—but they weathered them. Even with what felt like the whole world turning upside down, Zoom was able to stay steady.[26]

Steadiness like this requires rock-solid implementation.

WHY ARE WE TALKING IMPLEMENTATION?

You thought this book was about making decisions, right? Why are we devoting an entire chapter to what comes *after* you've made the decision?

People look at making a decision as a kind of end state. We made the decision! We're done! The truth is, high-impact decisions need to be executed through formal projects. There is a start date and an end date. Specific objectives, like the ones we outlined earlier when we discussed establishing success criteria for your decision, need to be met. The success criteria are your compass, but to implement the decision, you have to make sure you have the right people with the right experi-

---

25 Eric S. Yuan, "A Message to Our Users," *Zoom Blog*, April 1, 2020, https://blog.zoom. us/a-message-to-our-users/.

26 Zoom, "Zoom Video Communications Reports Fourth Quarter and Fiscal Year 2022 Financial Results," press release, February 28, 2022, https://investors.zoom.us/news-releases/ news-release-details/zoom-video-communications-reports-fourth-quarter-and-fiscal-1.

ence and that you're all working toward the same goal. It's a lot of moving parts, and if you don't get all the parts—and all the people—moving in the right direction, project logistics can get out of hand, very quickly.

The short answer is: we're devoting an entire chapter to implementation because you're not done when the decision is made. You're just getting started.

THE PROJECT MANAGEMENT TRIANGLE

For every implementation process, three constraints need to be considered:

Scope. That's the work associated with implementing the decision, including quality expectations.

Cost. This includes the budget, materials, and human resources (because if you don't have the internal resources, you may need to hire consultants/contractors).

Timeline. This is your schedule for implementation.

These three constraints form the Project Management Triangle.

The triple constraint theory states that whenever one leg of the triangle changes, at least one or both of the other legs have to change with it.

Let's say your timelines get cut in half. You have a well-balanced project management triangle. You already know this implementation is going to cost $10,000. It's going to take you ten months, and you've got five people working on it. Suddenly someone comes to you and says, *actually...you only have five months to get this done.* What do you need to make that happen?

You could cut the scope in half and work with the same people and resources to get it done. That will balance your triangle. Or, you could keep the same scope, cut the timelines in half, and then add a lot more resources. In this case, you'd need to go from a five-person project team to a ten-person project team.

Be constantly thinking about these kinds of trade-offs as you move through implementation.

A lot of people take on additional scope without controlling the changes (i.e., adjusting the schedule/cost legs of the triangle). It's called "scope creep," and it's very common. Scope creep puts you behind schedule and over budget, and it risks burnout among the people working on the implementation. Stay vigilant, keep your triangle balanced, and avoid scope creep.

CHANGE MANAGEMENT

On the project management side, you have to manage the technical aspects: scope, time, and cost. On the people side, you have to manage the *change*.

Change is hard. It doesn't matter if it's necessary change or wanted change...people react in powerful ways to change and it's during implementation those reactions have to be managed.

If you fail to communicate well, all the hard work on project management is going to go by the wayside. You can think of change like turbulence. Depending on how well the change is managed, it can feel to employees like light, moderate, or severe turbulence. Recognizing that there will always be some bumps when high-impact decisions are implemented, we want to avoid getting into moderate and severe turbulence, when at all possible.

- **Light turbulence** momentarily causes slight changes in altitude and/or attitude or a slight bumpiness. Occupants of the airplane may feel a slight strain against their seat belts.
- **Moderate turbulence** is similar to light turbulence but somewhat more intense. There is, however, no loss of control of the airplane. Occupants will feel a definite strain against their seat belts and unsecured objects will be dislodged.
- **Severe turbulence** causes large and abrupt changes in altitude and/or attitude and, usually, large variations in indicated airspeed. The airplane may momentarily be out of control. Occupants of the airplane will be forced violently against their seat belts.[27]

We've already spent a lot of time drilling into you the importance of communication. Nowhere is that more essential than here. When you put this decision in front of your decision-makers, you have to talk to them about the estimated cost and timeline. During implementation, your job, and theirs, is to

27 National Weather Service, "Turbulence," ZHU Training Page, accessed February 16, 2023, https://www.weather.gov/source/zhu/ZHU_Training_Page/turbulence_stuff/turbulence/turbulence.htm#:~:text=Turbulence%20Int[...]%20%20Extreme%20%20%20%20.

stick to those original agreements. Those are the boundaries you put in place.

You don't want to end up in a situation where you put in the work, did all the processes perfectly, made the right decisions, and then failed in hour two because you took your foot off the gas. If you focus on implementation as much as on decision-making, you are setting yourself up for success. If everyone understands the intent of what it is you're focusing on and trying to accomplish, then they can use that as a compass for their own decision-making. Communicate what you're trying to accomplish and what your success criteria are so that when any point changes on that project management triangle...you (and your team) will be prepared.

COMMUNICATION
ANNOUNCING A DECISION

When announcing a decision, start at the top with the executive level. Make sure everyone is on the same page. From there, you'll address your stakeholders. Be sure you have buy-in and everyone is fully aware of the announcement that's going to be made. It's very hard to encourage change from the bottom up within an organization. That means you need your executives on board, then your senior leadership, then your managers, and then all of the individual contributors before you make any kind of company-wide announcement.

Everyone should be talking the same talk and know what's going on. That way, when you do finally start to spread the word wide and employees start to ask their managers questions about the decision, they'll have answers.

Once you're ready to make the big announcement, don't let it get lost in a single, "Big News," email. A rule of thumb is that people should receive the information many times and in different forms of communication: verbal, all-hands meetings, one-on-one manager meetings, email, Slack, on your website, or any available channel. Connect with teams in all the different ways to spread the word. Repetition is how the message sticks...especially if the outcome of the decision will affect most, if not all, of the people in your organization. If you're rolling out a new payroll or a performance management system—one that everyone will be using—you want the announcement to come in clear and come in often.

The other important piece of this is the "why." In particular, if you've made a decision that is not aligned with a recommendation, people are going to be wondering, *why are we doing this?* You need to nail the why and you need to nail it right out of the gate. Don't give people any room to guess. Establish what is happening and *why* it's happening. Start at a high level, and drill down into the details about what it means for individual stakeholders based on the group of people you're addressing.

WHO'S ON YOUR TEAM?

The number of people you'll be communicating with will change based on the size of the project. For a smaller scale decision, you may need only one or two people to implement, but that team and routine need to get bigger as the implementation needs increase. For larger initiatives, you'll need larger teams. Depending on size, you'll need to go through all of the same steps, just at a different scale.

If you're buying a house, you'll have a few core team members: the realtor, the buyer, the seller, the title company, and the lender. All you will need to make that transaction happen are this tight-core team of experts. If you're making a payroll conversion to a new system for 25,000 employees, your team for implementation will be much larger, and the coordination that much more complex. In either scenario, you will need to make sure you understand what success looks like so that you're getting the right people to buy in and behave in a way that aligns with the decision.

IS THIS REALLY NECESSARY?

This is a lot of work. We know. Why take all this time and mental energy to tailor your messaging and get buy-in from each group? Your decision's been made! People will get on board. Right?

Wrong.

If you don't do the leg work, your initiative (and the thousands or millions of dollars invested in it) might fail. It's very likely that it *will fail*. You need buy-in and advocates on your side pre-launch, and simultaneous with launch.

You thought you were done after you made the decision? You're not finished until you have *adoption*.

Think of your teams—all the involved parties—like runners going around a track. Some of them are going to sprint; those are your early adopters. Then you're going to have the people who are just cruising along, chatting, walking at a clip, but definitely not running to get there. Some of them are walking off the track entirely to get a hot dog and coming back just in time to see people crossing the finish line. *"How was it?"* They're going to ask them, *"How did you feel?"* Your decision isn't implemented until you get *all* these people across the finish line.

That's why you may want to come up with some tactics for helping them go from a stroll to a jog.

KNOW YOUR AUDIENCE

Research has shown that middle managers are one of the groups most resistant to change. Often you'll see executives or project teams making a decision and rolling it out all at once. This is a mistake. If you don't get those middle managers on board, the ones that have all of the individual contributors reporting to them, that's a big swing and a miss. You'll introduce resistance.

Communicate early, often, and more specifically, the closer you get to the change.

Remember Damon's story about moving from physical to digital manuals at Learnit? The instructors were like those middle managers, an important and necessary group of stakeholders within the organization. They saw the change as only beneficial to Learnit, but not to them. When Damon was able to talk Jim Olay through the transition, Jim was able to make the leap and come to an understanding, unprompted by Damon, of how the new digital manuals would benefit the instructors and their students. By having Jim as an influencer and someone on their side, he was able to relay the benefits to his peers and get buy-in. This wasn't just a corporate-only decision; there really was value for the people most directly affected.

COMMUNICATE WIIFM

You have to target the stakeholders you're communicating with and again think about their WIIFM. We brought up the, "What's in it for me?" question in Chapter Eight when we talked about gaining buy-in. Here you're going to use the empathy you developed, thinking through this question for key stakeholders, and communicate the benefits. Think about this for each group you're addressing. Damon's messaging for instructors had to be different than for the executives or the students. WIIFM is about the benefits that the specific group cares most about. You can manage resistance by taking a bit of an imaginative journey and trying to predict what they might push back on.

Take advantage of your key influencers. Jim Olay was the right person to go to because he had sway—he was well-liked. When in the implementation phase, consider getting early adopters to pilot or test your initiative so that they can see the benefits with their own eyes and communicate with their peers. That kind of peer-to-peer recommendation carries so much more weight than any messaging coming from the project team. Early adopters, pilots, and influencers are your "change advocates." Use them.

Key customers can also be change advocates. If you're rolling out a new product or service, look to these customers for input. Make them feel they are part of the process because if they do, chances are they will advocate for you as well.

As you're coming up with your communications plan, put yourself in the other person's shoes—whether it's your internal teams, your external influencers, or your customers—ask yourself, what questions will they have? Even a well-thought-out FAQ can go a long way. Knowing your audience's pain points and addressing them head-on is so much more powerful than a few canned sentences shared indiscriminately.

RESISTANCE MANAGEMENT AND TRAINING

Expect resistance when change is coming. It's natural. A big part of resistance can be managed through transparent communication, although you may need to take additional steps. Your key influencers can help. If they're out there mingling, working the room, they can gather useful intel about people's concerns and bring it back to the project team. Once you understand where the resistance is coming from, you can think through ways to get people on board. It's proactive objection handling.

Let's take a real-life example.

Kandis has new headphones. They're big and fancy. They're Bluetooth-connected, wireless, and they have ten hours of battery life! These are excellent, game-changing, headphones. The other day, Kandis got her first chance to try them out. She was walking through the airport and she got a call from a client.

Hooray, new headphones!

She pulled them out of her bag and put them on. No connection. She asked the client to hold on while she fiddled around, pressing buttons, and trying to get the Bluetooth to work. She couldn't even tell if the damn things were on or off. After a couple minutes, she threw them back in her bag, frustrated, and pulled out her old crummy headphones, which she hates. The batteries always die before she's even finished with her phone call, but at least she knows how to use them!

Kandis was frustrated with the change. She knows, deep down, that if she keeps using her new headphones, she'll figure them out. She'll learn *beep beep beep* means they're connected. She also knows that it's easy to revert to old ways because they're comfortable. These are the kinds of frustrations people encounter when they're going through change.

Give people the time and the resources to figure out those new headphones. Otherwise, they are just going to rifle through their backpack...and out will come the old, inferior ones. People like to do what's comfortable, and they'll continue to do it—unless you support them through the change.

CULTURE AND CHANGE

If your organization has been able to build a culture of growth mindset, you are well positioned for change. If you don't know what a "growth mindset" is, ask a seven-year-old. It's probably on posters all over their classroom.

Growth mindset is all about how you view challenges and setbacks. People with a growth mindset (versus a "fixed mindset") believe that even if they struggle with certain skills, their abilities aren't static. With work, they can improve.

At Microsoft, they call these kinds of people "lifelong learners." In a growth mindset culture, people are constantly learning and developing. They feel okay being vulnerable and making mistakes. Many organizations struggle to develop an environment that is conducive to this way of being. If you don't have a growth mindset culture, or if you work with a team who is resistant to change, you may have to supplement or replace existing team members with people who are more open to trying and failing.

This kind of outlook starts at the top. If you have leadership who is excited about change, who knows that things don't always go as planned, and who is comfortable making a mistake and admitting it, then other people are also going to feel emboldened to stick their necks out and take a chance.

No one wants to be the Blockbuster of the moment. Or Kodak. You want to be able to change with the times. You want to be Zoom.

Zoom's founder and CEO, Eric Yuan, was a big part of several other companies before he came to Zoom. These were big-name companies: WebEx, and Cisco. In those organizations, he said, they focused on technology, but customers weren't happy. When he talks about Zoom, his tune is very different.

"From the moment we founded Zoom, our main focus has

been to provide a cloud video communications solution that would make customers happy. That focus has continued to guide all our innovations, partnerships, and other initiatives. The fantastic growth we're experiencing and the many industry accolades we've received can all be attributed to having satisfied customers that enjoy using our platform."

"Our biggest accomplishment," he went on to say, "is creating a culture of happiness at Zoom."

They value happy customers. That is their metric for success. As they implement new technology, they keep coming back to this touchstone. *What do our end users think about this? Are they happy?* They course correct along the way, based on these responses.

If you have a growth mindset in your culture, then you won't be afraid to say, "You know what? This didn't quite work. Our customers aren't happy. Let's do it a different way."

Change requires people who are willing to make mistakes.

Instead of embodying a "my way or the highway" attitude (which, sadly, is much more common), Zoom is constantly focused on customers and what their feedback is. They've referenced this guiding principle when talking about the free version of Zoom as well. They had so much faith in people's appreciation for their product that they gave it away for free. They had confidence that people would eventually upgrade to other features because they loved the product so much.

EXECUTIVE SPONSORSHIP

Remember: change can't happen from the bottom up. Leaders need to be walking the walk (and talking the talk) first. During change management, you need to have a sponsor. Someone high up the chain, who has name recognition. When Learnit rolls out any new initiative, Damon is out front as the sponsor. He lets people know what's changing, how and why, and that he, as an executive, is one thousand percent supportive of the change. He also makes it clear that he expects that everyone will get on board.

On the project management side, a sponsor is someone who can escalate issues as they arise. The executive sponsor will be there to request additional funds or more resources, or to adjust the support in anyway necessary.

If you roll out a big initiative, and the senior executives don't come out of the gate excited and supportive, the rest of the organization is going to wonder, *why should we be?*

CHANGE ADOPTION

Not all implementations will require change, but for anything that is system-focused or involves a new process, you will want to ask yourself what knowledge and ability you need to instill in people so that they are set up for success.

Think about it this way: if you were an individual contributor at an organization, and you got promoted to a management role, guess what? You'd walk out of work one day as a contributor and walk in the next day as a manager. You'd, overnight, have a different job, and when that happens you are going to need skills to help you be successful in that new role.

When Learnit conducts management training, they focus on these kinds of skills. Here's how you give specific feedback. Here's how you set up a meeting with your employees. Here's what you should be talking about, in that meeting.

The same kind of detailed training is required when people in your organization are going through any kind of change. Meet them where they're at. Find out, if you don't know already, what's going to support them most in their being able to make this change. This could mean formal training, going through modules that will cover what they need to know to be successful with this change. It could mean online training, or a printed manual, or a live demonstration. Or you could set up office hours where people can come and ask questions about the change.

People learn in different ways. Some people are visual learners, some people prefer a checklist. Offer different avenues and different ways to train people in situations where it's necessary. Whether it's learning modules, peer-to-peer exercises, or even coaching, you need to make sure that people can get the help that they need.

This goes back to the culture of a growth mindset. You can lead a dog to water, as the old saying goes, but you can't make him drink. Initiatives fail when teams have a fixed mindset. All the support and training in the world aren't going to help that. Before you invest time and money in training for change, make sure you have the right people with the right mindset, on board.

For those of you who are visual learners, we're including here our Change Management Worksheet. You can also access it on our website at: https://www.kandisanddamon.com/book.

Change Management Worksheet

DECISION NAME –

IMPLEMENTOR –

PURPOSE OF DECISION –

Describe the decision and *why* it is needed. What benefits will it bring? Will it increase revenue? Will it make processes more efficient? What happens without this decision?

PICTURE OF SUCCESS –

What does the future look like with a successful outcome, after the decision is implemented?

KEY CONTRIBUTIONS FROM LEADERS –

Tip: Messaging that includes business needs should come from senior leaders and how the change will impact specific people should come from supervisors.

Action / Message			
Timeline:		**Responsible Party:**	[Name] Senior Leader / Supervisor
Action / Messaging			

ADDITIONAL COMMUNICATIONS:

Communication No. 1			
Audience:		Delivery Method:	
Responsible to Draft:			
Responsible to Distribute:			
Delivery Timeline:			
Message:			

TRAINING – What are the needs?

Training			
Audience:		Delivery Method:	
Responsible to Create:			
Responsible to Deliver:			
Delivery Timeline:			
Training Objectives:			

RESISTANCE MANAGEMENT – What actions need taken? (e.g., office hours, town hall, etc.)

Resistance Management Plan	
Audience:	
Timeline:	
Detailed Approach:	

BE LIKE ZOOM

Change is hard. It's worth saying again.

When Zoom not only weathered global change but grew by many multiples, it wasn't just about smart decision-making. They paid attention to what mattered—their *people*. They had a growth mindset and they adjusted as they got feedback. They weren't afraid to course correct, and they let everyone know what they were doing and why they were doing it. Most importantly, they understood what their success metric was (customer happiness) and they never strayed from it.

Zoom had many large-scale implementations over the

course of its explosive growth, and it managed to make it look effortless from the customer perspective...though it wasn't without its challenges. Early on in the pandemic, a host in a Zoom meeting had the ability to unmute anyone in the room, at anytime. This led to some pretty embarrassing moments, for hosts and participants. Zoom heard from end users that this feature wasn't great. To mitigate this, they added an extra layer of security. Now, if someone tries to unmute you while you're on Zoom, there's a popup that appears and says that you've been requested to unmute. You have to click your acceptance. They got feedback, and they course corrected.

From a user perspective, though, Zoom just works. Yes, there are features that change and will continue to, but as a video conferencing tool, it works. They have not been known to have periods where servers are down and the system is inaccessible. This means that they were able to successfully plan and support the customers they were taking on, as they took them on.

When issues arose, especially around security, they owned up to them. When "Zoom bombers" were jumping into meetings they hadn't been invited to and causing trouble, Zoom sent an email to all its customers letting them know what was happening and how they could protect themselves. Zoom was ahead of the problem, tapped in from their many feedback sources, and they were able to address it, head-on, with new security measures.

Their implementation strategy has allowed Zoom to become known as a responsive, supportive, and competent company.

We wish the same for you.

STEP RECAP...

Before we move on, let's recap the most important elements and action items in this step.

STEP SEVEN: IMPLEMENTATION

Many books on decision-making end with the decision. We deliberately chose not to do that, since we've seen so many decisions fail in implementation. The decision is ultimately only as strong as its results, and its results are as strong as its implementation.

Change is hard for people. If you do not think through the change step-by-step and explain what's in it for them, it will not go well. People on the impacted end will need to be helped through the change with training, office hours, and a huge amount of communication. The most technically sound rollout in the world will fail if the people who matter are not on board.

Don't sugarcoat. If a decision has to be made because of reasons that are not great, be transparent about that. People aren't dumb, and they will disengage if they sense there is more to the story than they're being told. They will need to be told why they should change in a way that makes sense to them.

The people side is important, and so is the technical side of implementation. Even if all of the people are on board, if the project requires more money and time than expected, or if the technology fails, the decision fails too.

WHAT'S NEXT?

Now that you've implemented, it's time to ask: *how do I measure progress?* How do you know whether you've succeeded or failed? We'll tackle this together in the next chapter.

CHAPTER ELEVEN

STEP EIGHT

MEASURE PROGRESS

PELOTON INTERACTIVE STARTED IN 2012. THEIR FOCUS was on bringing the community and excitement of boutique fitness into the home. In 2013, they raised $307,332 in a crowd-funding campaign. They used those funds to create an indoor exercise bike. In 2019, the company went public and raised more than $1.1 billion at a $29 per share price. During the COVID pandemic, their stock went through the roof. In December 2020, their price per share was $167.72. Little wonder. People were forced to stay at home due to state and city restrictions, and Peloton was giving them access to an online community of like-minded fitness enthusiasts. Peloton's indoor bike replaced the workouts they now no longer had access to. People couldn't get enough.

Peloton spent loads of money increasing production and the number of warehouses. They turned a blind eye to the reality that eventually the world would open back up again. Gyms would be accessible. Demand was going to decrease; it was just a matter of time.

In 2019, Peloton bought a manufacturing plant in Taiwan. In 2020, they spent $420M to acquire Precor, a fitness equipment maker. They had plans to build an additional $400M factory in Ohio, though those were eventually scrapped. These decisions helped them meet demand at the peak of the pandemic, but did they really evaluate all the alternatives? What kinds of future scenarios did they play out?

By May of 2021, Peloton's stock had dropped to $83.81.

In February 2022, Barry McCarthy became Peloton's CEO, replacing John Foley amid months of company turmoil.

"They spent money on things that they shouldn't have," McCarthy said. "They got caught up in the vision thing at the expense of getting real." The new CEO halted production and more than 2,800 employees were laid off due to a "restructuring program."

"This restructuring program is the result of diligent planning to address key areas of the business and realign our operations so that we can execute against our growth opportunity with efficiency and discipline," Peloton commented in a press release.

After only four months with their new CEO, Peloton stocks were at an all-time low. This wasn't due to new leadership but rather to many of their pandemic decisions catching up with them. But they weren't done yet. By September 2022, Peloton stock was less than seven dollars a share.

We don't bring up this example to delight in anyone's misery. Peloton may recover. With the course correction instituted by new leadership, hopefully, they will. As of this writing, their stock has already risen by many percentage points.

The point is, you must always be in the position to course correct and change direction. If a decision that was previously made is no longer meeting the intent, reevaluate. If the landscape has changed, rethink. A decision that may have led to great success earlier, may need to change at a later date. Keep your finger on the pulse. Have success metrics to keep your eye on what matters.

MEASURING PROGRESS

When revisiting a decision, you need objective criteria to measure success. The bottom-line question is: was the intent of the decision met, or not? Even if you did the best you could, and made the best possible decision, there's still a chance that intent was not met. You may need to go back to an earlier step of the decision-making process.

During implementation, you work to get people to buy in. You make sure they are doing what they need to be doing to make the decision a success. At this point in the process, you will look at the fruits of these labors. Was it adopted? Was your decision successful? Implementation is all about trying to get people across the finish line; measuring progress is about declaring a *winner*. As Peter Drucker, a famous management guru, says, "What gets measured, gets managed."

If everything is important, nothing is important. The metrics you will use to measure success are the most important aspects of your decision and will get the most attention.

When you use your metrics they should align with the metrics themselves. This means you might have a metric that says you want to be at a certain place in six months, and again in nine months. You should have a roadmap that indicates not only whether you were successful right after the decision was implemented, but also further down the line. Did it grow roots and become a part of company culture? Was it sustained?

Let's say you're trying to improve employee engagement—a goal at the top of many minds these days Everyone is burned out from the COVID-19 pandemic. Employee engagement is driving one of your decisions. You did an employee engagement survey and can see that 60 percent of the people in your company feel engaged. You want to make a decision that will improve that. You come up with an option for a hybrid work schedule where people will have some days at the office and some days at home to help them maintain work-life balance.

You go through the entire process. You design what that schedule will look, and feel like, and you implement it. Then, you measure progress. Six months out, you take another survey. You know that one of your success metrics was to move that 60 percent engagement number to 85 percent. When you hand out your second survey, you know that's what you want to see: a 25 percent increase in engagement. You get the surveys back, and your number is 87 percent. Congratulations! You did it!

- **Baseline:** 60 percent engagement
- **Goal:** 85 percent engagement in six months
- **Results:** 87 percent engagement at the six-month point

Well, hang on.

If you don't nurture and keep paying attention to that engagement, six more months down the road, that number could be 50 percent. It's never "one and done" when it comes to high-impact decisions.

Define what success looks like on an ongoing basis. Have metrics that can continue to be measured, so that you know when to course correct. Come up with metrics for different operational departments so that continued success is on many different radars.

The key to being successful in this step is to define your success metrics early in the process and measure them along the way. You also need to communicate these metrics to your team and help them understand why it is important. You don't want to have to play catch-up. If you make a decision to implement a new payroll system and one of your metrics is that you want to have 95 percent of employees set up in the system by a certain date, that is a measurable success metric. On that date, you'll look at the metrics and see if you are at 95 percent or not. If not, then what do you need to do? You'll go back to implementing, supporting people, reinforcing the change, and making sure they know how to log into the system.

There are more cycles than straight lines. You may be measuring progress at certain points, then returning to support people who are impacted by the decision, and then back to measuring progress again. Sometimes it's simultaneous. You'll be progressing in sprints. You'll implement, measure, close it out, and move on to the next.

Without success metrics, it will be nearly impossible to measure your progress. If you have found yourself in a situation where the success metrics are ill-defined or nonexistent, look to your team. Get the right people in the room. Remember your DIDI: Decision-maker, those providing Input, the Driver, and Implementers. Go back to the beginning and figure out the intent of the decision. Brainstorm objective criteria you can apply right away.

If you are implementing a decision for an organization that is investing in the project or has shareholders that report to a board, they are going to want to know what success looks like in numbers. If you've hit the numbers, great. Toot your own horn. If you haven't, put your ego to one side and tell them what you plan to do and how you plan to get there.

TRY, TRY, AGAIN

You can change course but don't give up on the intent of your decision. If you need to, go back to the drawing board on options. Maybe you didn't select the correct path to get to your success metrics. If the road you went down didn't take you where you wanted to go, flip it into reverse. Go back to where the road splits and try the other way. There are almost always other options. Ask yourself what else you can do. *What other path can you take?*

Sometimes you make a good decision and it is derailed by factors totally outside of your control. During the pandemic, the cost of materials skyrocketed. People had to change their operating models because of it. Peloton did everything they could to increase production (at a high cost!) based on the immediate demand. Everyone and their mom wanted to buy a Peloton bike. Then fast-forward to when gyms opened back up and suddenly Peloton has incredible overhead and quickly decreasing demand.

At the time, Peloton may have felt they were making a great decision. There was a huge demand, and they met it. Months later, they were going bankrupt. In hindsight, they made a bad call. Maybe if they had a success metric in place that considered sustainability long term, they might have thought differently.

The market is going to keep changing. There will be new events, new information, and new crises. Success will need to be measurable, over the long term, if you want your decision to have a lasting impact. Sometimes the path you started down was the right path, but when internal or external factors change, you have to be willing to reassess. Don't let the cost fallacy lead you astray. Even if you've invested a ton of money and resources, if you're not getting closer to your success criteria, it's time to change course.

Ego and pride won't serve you well here. Be flexible. Create a trusting environment to have hard conversations. Be willing to learn from your success and your failures.

GROWTH MINDSET, AGAIN

Failure sucks. That is a universal truth. There is, however, a great dividing line between people who get stuck in failure and those who can learn from their missteps. Talk to yourself using the language that Carol Dweck developed around a growth mindset:

We're not there...yet. We tried, and it didn't turn out. That's okay. We'll get through this challenge.

If you have a culture of growth mindset you can avoid playing the blame game. People with fixed mindsets are the first to point a finger when decisions go wrong. If you have a culture of blame, people aren't going to want to go out there and innovate. They're going to do exactly what's expected of them, and no more.

A growth mindset leads to flexibility in decision-making. If you see that a project you're implementing isn't going in the right direction, you don't have to stubbornly continue down the path. You don't need to get all the way to the end before you decide whether it was a good decision or a bad one. You can pause at any point and examine. Then you'll be able to shift your course of action sooner rather than later. It takes trust to do that.

Risk is always in the future, remember, and may or may not occur. If it does, it could negatively or positively affect your project or initiative. Empowering people within your organization to be proactive rather than reactive is critical. If we're reactive, negative risk is going to be realized and become an issue. You are going to be focused on addressing those issues, and putting out fires, rather than thinking forward. If we're proactive, we are going to identify risks in advance, analyze them, and develop a plan to mitigate them, preventing them from becoming an issue.

Instead of just looking at what could go wrong, ask yourself what could go *right*. What positive outcome could we take advantage of?

KNOW YOUR ODDS

Annie Duke, the world champion poker player, makes the point in her book, *Thinking in Bets*, that life is more like poker than like chess. No matter how carefully and well we play the board, there is always an element of luck. Events happen that are outside our control. Don't hold yourself accountable for circumstances you have no control over.

When we talk about risk, we are really talking about two things: probability, which is usually a percentage multiplied by impact, and time or money. What's the probability of this particular project going wrong, and if it does go wrong, what's the impact? You may have to pay X amount of dollars more than you budgeted or delay your project for six months.

Think about it like gambling. If you're going to the poker table, you want to know what the chances are that the dealer is going to lay down hearts. There are fifty-two cards in a deck— thirteen of each suit (hearts, spades, clubs, diamonds). That means there's a 25 percent chance you'll get a heart. Use this kind of percentage when you're defining risk. If there's a 25 percent chance you'll get a heart, that means there's a 75 percent chance you will get a spade, diamond, or club. Is it worth it to you to take the bet? Make sure you consider the impact when making the decision. Even with a 25 percent chance that you will get a heart, the reward may be worth taking the bet.

Putting percentages on risk allows you to prioritize the ones that are more likely to happen and look at the impact. You need to be looking and thinking about both—probability and impact—when you're thinking in bets.

When you're looking back into the past and trying to figure out whether or not you made a good decision, percentages will allow you to determine what made you unsuccessful. You can see, *was this even on our radar?* If there was a 75 percent chance an event was going to occur that would negatively impact your project and it wasn't flagged in earlier steps, there are going to be some hard questions to answer about why.

Pay attention to what is going on internally in your organization, and externally, in the world at large. Humans tend to attribute success to personal decisions and failure to luck. (Isn't that convenient?) Go back through your timeline and make sure success was a success and not luck. Look at your failures and find out where the responsibility really lies. Take honest stock and make necessary corrections from there.

OUR CHANGING WORLD

This doesn't just apply to high-impact decisions at work.

As of the writing of this book, there are gigantic shifts taking place in the housing market. People are desperate to buy homes. They may have been approved for a loan and locked in at an interest rate that is only good for ninety days. Maybe they have been shopping but are outbid at every turn. When that interest rate expires, it will be subject to the market. In a normal market that might be fine, but currently, average mortgage interest rates have ballooned to the highest in close to fifteen years.

If you were looking in the $600,000 range for a house and your interest rate suddenly went from 3.5 percent to 6.5 percent, that would have a huge impact on your buying power. You might suddenly find yourself looking for a $500,000 house. You might decide, you know what, too rich for my blood. You might get out of the market altogether. There are so many moving parts that can make a decision successful or unsuccessful; be mindful of all of them.

Nurture your willingness to adapt and react in real-time. If you remain rigid just for the sake of staying on course, you're going to be less successful in the long run. Our world, our organizations, and our personal lives are constantly changing. Technology continues to advance. AI is creeping into more and more of our daily experiences. Pandemics will continue to happen. We're not living at the same pace our parents and grandparents did. No longer can you just make a plan and stick to it.

ORGANIZATIONAL AGILITY

Agility starts at the top. If you want to grow an agile organization, your processes need to be lean yet effective. Empower people to make suggestions and embrace good ones quickly. If every decision has to funnel to the top for approval, you'll end up with a bottleneck. Empower your teams from the top of the organization, all the way down. Give boundaries and guidance about what they're empowered to make decisions on, but let them have the freedom to move in the right direction.

To do that, you'll have to make your strategic goals and objectives transparent. Leaders need to be communicating them and cascading them down through the different organizational levels. For the million little decisions that aren't high-impact but still steer the ship, give people the knowledge and authority to implement them. These "baby step" decisions have a huge impact on your organization in the long run. Make sure everyone is clear on, and shares, the same long-term vision.

Agility also means being willing to go back to the drawing board, no matter how invested you were in a previous plan. For Peloton, having maximum manufacturing power for their bikes was good for a certain period. When demand disappeared, that choice required reexamining. They could have course corrected, right then and there. They could have leased out some of their manufacturing facilities. They could have closed them immediately. You need agility to look at what's important and evaluate and acknowledge when you're not moving in the right direction.

You don't have to make this up as you go. There are questions you and your team can ask as a decision is being implemented, to evaluate progress and ensure you're on the right track. This way, you can either remain on course or anticipate the need for corrective action.

These questions are:

1. Are any milestones being missed or delayed?
2. Are the resources and budget being managed efficiently?
3. Are stakeholders/customers satisfied with the progress?
4. Is the decision still in line with the overall organizational goals?
5. Has anything changed in the internal or external environment that should lead us to reevaluate?

By routinely assessing the progress of the implementation, it is possible to take corrective measures as needed and ensure that you remain on course. Even if you have to make a few hairpin turns along the way.

RIP MR. BIG

In case you haven't heard, Mr. Big is dead. He died in the very first episode of the Sex and the City reboot, "And Just Like That." Don't worry, Carrie's going to be just fine. It's Peloton you should feel sorry for.

In the heart-wrenching penultimate scene, Mr. Big (the infamous eternal flame to Sarah Jessica Parker's, Carrie Bradshaw) has a heart attack while riding his Peloton bike and dies. Peloton was reportedly unaware of the plot twist. Shares of their stock plunged over 16 percent in the two days following the episode's release. If that's not bad luck, we don't know what is.

A beloved character from a beloved show dying while using your product is not an outcome Peloton could have ever predicted. It was, most likely, a huge surprise. It was a moment of bad luck, but the response is the same. When faced with a bad outcome, it's time to dig in. Get your trusted team in the room and figure out what's next.

STEP RECAP...

Before we move on, let's recap the most important elements and action items in this step.

STEP EIGHT: ASSESSING THE DECISION

After you implement the decision, it's important to come back and assess whether you made the right decision. That way, you can learn from both mistakes and successes and your next decision will get better.

There's no hard-and-fast rule for how long to wait after the implementation before you assess. It will depend on the decision. For example, if you hire a new salesperson, you won't know if that's a good decision for six months or more. You may have some clues at three months, but not enough. In contrast, if you're testing a new online ads campaign, you might be able to have solid data on your decision within three days.

In all cases, though, you'll need to return to your original criteria and intent to see if you've been successful. What were the results you were looking for? Did you accomplish those results?

WHAT'S NEXT?

By this point you should be well acquainted with your metrics for success, and hopefully ready to go out there and start making some decisions.

This book is intended to be a framework for helping you do exactly that. Use it in your organization or your life. We hope it will help you, but like any framework, it will need to be modified for the decision at hand. Course correction applies to us too.

We intend that this book can be one tool in your toolbox. Use the process as a template, and bend it to your needs. When you're narrowing down your options, utilize the decision-making matrix. Keep a growth mindset. Stay agile, and don't be afraid to make mistakes.

CONCLUSION

DECISION-MAKING CAN BE HARD AND MESSY, PARTICU-larly when it comes to high-stakes decisions. An effective process and strong tools (like the ones in this book) make it easier.

A formal decision-making process challenges your assumptions and emotional shortcuts. It forces you to think more critically, and more broadly. It breaks you out of the trap of binary thinking and creates more and better options. It prevents surprises.

It's easy to just go with your gut, but especially with high-impact decision-making that inevitably leads to regret. You spend less time deciding, but more time dealing with the pain and anxiety that arises. You'll be cleaning up messes more than charting your course.

If instead, you do a better job going through the process, it takes longer. There is more legwork and more attention to detail. You're forced to do the exhausting work of critical thinking. You have copious conversations with all of your stakeholders. It's hard.

While there's no guarantee that the outcome will be perfect, going through the process does avoid foreseeable traps. If there are other people affected by a decision, a clear process aids buy-in and implementation. It creates opportunities to think and communicate clearly.

A REVIEW OF THE BOOK

To help you cement what you've learned about decision-making, let's review everything we've talked about so far.

AVOID COMMON DECISION-MAKING FAILURES

Bad decisions often follow well-worn bad habits.

Emotional and reactive decision-making is by far the worst. You will want to break this habit, to get ahead of major decisions, and use a considered process. By making decisions out of your prefrontal cortex rather than your limbic system, you'll be more likely to consider important consequences.

Analysis paralysis is a terrible habit as well. Many people become paralyzed and unable to act when they face an important decision and do not know what to do next. Freezing shows a lack of leadership and confidence and tends to self-reinforce. No decision *is a decision,* and normally the worst one. The best response to analysis paralysis is often a process. It makes your next step clear, and easier to take action on. This one shift alone will improve outcomes.

Confirmation bias, sunk cost bias, availability biases, and anchoring biases are all places where your brain will take a shortcut and destroy a decision. Be aware of and double-check your decisions against these to ensure you don't fall for the common traps.

Break your bad habits, and your decisions will improve. Of course, there's more to good decision-making than avoiding mistakes. You will need to actively add positive practices and strategies to make excellent decisions, especially when it comes to high-impact issues.

UNDERSTAND THE PSYCHOLOGY

Everyone has their own unique personality, and each personality has strengths and weaknesses. Your tendencies will inform how you naturally approach decisions, and self-awareness is key. Having a realistic idea of your limitations helps you compensate for them.

It's generally better to lean into your strengths and deliberately make up for your limitations. You can do this by deliberately going through a process and operating out of other preferences. Perhaps even better, you can collaborate with other people who have strengths that complement yours.

Again, self-awareness leads directly to success. You can surround yourself with people who are strong in areas where you know you are not. Do what you are best at, and depend on others to balance that out in other areas.

MAKE DECISION ROLES CLEAR

You've likely gone to a meeting where a decision is needed and no one makes it. You leave the meeting and there is no decision. No one took ownership, and no one researches for more information afterward. Without a clear understanding of roles, decision-making is messy at best and impossible at worst.

Every part of a decision is impacted by who is playing what role in that decision. Set yourself and your team up for success by making decision roles clear. Tell Roberto you want him to drive the decision and research the task. Tell him Margot will be deciding, but his recommendation as to the final three options will be key. Make the ownership of each role clear.

Also, make it clear *how* the decision will be decided. If there will be one final decision-maker, great. If everyone will be voting, that's also fine. The important thing is that everyone understands. We also recommend using this opportunity to set expectations around the decision in general. "We want to hear what you say during the process. You will absolutely have a chance to speak and give your input. Once the decision is made, though, everyone will need to get behind the decision and do their best to execute it. Can I count on you to do that?"

Failure to communicate roles and expectations leads to anger from the team. It will undermine the decision and its execution more quickly than just about any other mistake.

Learn your role and others' roles so that you know who is doing what.

THE EIGHT STEPS TO BETTER DECISION-MAKING:

- Step One: Define Decision and Successful Outcomes
- Step Two: Gather Information
- Step Three: Identify Options
- Step Four: Prioritize Options
- Step Five: Gain Buy-In
- Step Six: Make the Decision
- Step Seven: Implement the Decision
- Step Eight: Review the Decision

MEASUREMENTS

In most cases, you won't be able to point to one metric to determine whether the decision succeeded or failed. It may make sense to watch a metric (or several) over time. For example, if the goal is to implement a new payroll system within twelve months, you might measure that success in terms of quarterly milestones. Perhaps you will go live at the end of the first quarter. At the end of the second quarter, you need 30 percent of people to be registered in the system. By the third, 50 percent, and by the fourth, 97 percent of the people will need to have fully transitioned and confirmed the accuracy of their information.

Measurements can be set based on people, or based on technical goals. The idea is that the numbers help you assess whether success has been achieved. Focus on a few key indicators. (If everything is important, nothing is important.)

If you handled your intent well, there should be no question. You'll either have achieved the outcome, or not. Depending on the outcome, though, you may or may not be able to measure it more precisely than that. Not all outcomes are numerical.

LEARNING FROM THE DECISION

If you did not achieve the outcome, we recommend that you go through a full post-mortem exercise. Get together, not to point fingers but to identify blind spots and what you could have done differently. For a successful decision, see if you can identify why it was successful and what you can replicate in similar situations.

In both cases, though, keep in mind that there is an element of luck to outcomes. You can take all the right steps with the information you have and get a bad result, or make a sloppy decision and get a good result. (Though these outcomes are less likely.) To the degree that you can tease out luck, do that as well. If you failed in implementation, face that honestly. Assess the decision as well as you can, so that you can learn from it. Approach the situation carefully, though, so that you don't learn the wrong lessons from a result if the process wasn't great.

Once you assess the situation in terms of what was luck and what was skill, you're in a position to determine the next steps. If you should continue along your same course, great. If you messed up, or need to make another decision, you can always return to a previous step in the process.

Course correction is always an option.

YOU CAN DO THIS

This process for high-impact decision-making ensures that you're driven by logic and consideration. It protects you from the worst flaws of emotional and impulsive decision-making. It widens your options and creates stronger, healthier decisions with generally better outcomes. It will take time, but that time will pay off easily in the long run.

Decision-making around high-impact decisions is hard. It can be emotionally draining, and messy. However, the more you do it, the easier it will get. Your experience will speak volumes, and you can move forward with confidence.

The process is worth it. After you make a few high-impact decisions using this framework, you'll see your outcomes improve overall. You'll step into positive results across your work and life. Good decisions really do equal success.

We will say that no process is perfect off the shelf. Consider this book a guide, not a prescription. You will want to tailor anything and everything in it for your situation. Make every tool work for *you*.

IMPROVING YOUR DECISION-MAKING SKILLS

Leaders spend 40 percent of their time making decisions.[28] That's almost half their working hours. Personal decisions are no less taxing. Because of this demand, decision-making should be considered a critical skill. Invest time in improving it. Work to get better over time.

The information in this book will be helpful, but there are also other frameworks and tools you can use. We recommend continuing to study a wide variety of resources, and to apply them deliberately to your decisions. Continue to assess the results of your decisions, and continue to apply what you learn to the decisions you make in the future.

You don't have to be perfect at this skill to see better results. You can learn by experience and by practice. You will have to make many decisions in your work and life. Why not do so deliberately? Why not learn the skill in more depth as you go? There are so many opportunities for honing your skills, week by week and year by year.

You can do this, and it will get easier over time.

ORGANIZATIONAL DECISION-MAKING

Organizations have special needs and problems when it comes to decision-making. If you don't have the in-house expertise needed to bring a high-impact decision to fruition, this is where it is worth considering bringing in experts like Kandis and Damon who specialize in these skills. By tapping into their expertise, your team can gain valuable insights and strategies

---

28 "Make Faster, Better Decisions," McKinsey & Company, accessed March 24, 2023, https://www.mckinsey.com/capabilities/people-and-organizational-performance/our-insights/make-faster-better-decisions?cid=app.

for making effective decisions that are based on data, analysis, and a deep understanding of your organization's goals and priorities.

Kandis and Damon have helped organizations overcome challenges associated with a leadership team getting stuck in the boardroom trying to reach a consensus (versus having another plan for getting across the finish line in making decisions), solving the wrong problem, or having confusion in decision-making roles.

Contact us to explore tackling a project together!

GOOD DECISIONS EQUAL SUCCESS

We've all made decisions we wish we could take back. We've sent emails that we wish we didn't write. Deciding from emotion can lead to huge surprises, regret, financial loss, and more.

For high-stakes decisions, you need more than your gut; you need critical thinking and formal decision-making tools. They help you identify risk more easily, and help identify second-and third-level consequences of the decision. Never underestimate the power of critical thinking.

After all, good decisions equal success.